500 Classroom Tips
Grades K–1

Table of Contents

500 Classroom Tips
Grades K–1

About This Book

Looking for creative ideas to get organized and add some fresh appeal to your classroom routines? We've got 500 of them just for you! Whether you're a first-year or seasoned teacher, this idea-packed resource is your guide to creating and maintaining a motivating and productive classroom. We've collected the best classroom-tested ideas from *The Mailbox®* magazine and conveniently organized them into one comprehensive package. Inside you'll quickly and easily find surefire suggestions on the timely topics you need most!

- Classroom Routines and Events
- Organizational Tips
- Curriculum Ties and Lesson Helps
- Student Motivation and Work Management
- Communication

Managing Editor: Allison E. Ward

Editorial Team: Becky S. Andrews, Kimberley Bruck, Karen P. Shelton, Diane Badden, Cayce Guiliano, Susan Walker, Kimberly A. Brugger, Cindy Daoust, Leanne Stratton, Karen A. Brudnak, Sarah Hamblet, Hope Rodgers, Dorothy C. McKinney

Production Team: Lisa K. Pitts, Pam Crane, Clevell Harris, Rebecca Saunders, Jennifer Tipton Bennett, Chris Curry, Theresa Lewis Goode, Ivy L. Koonce, Clint Moore, Greg D. Rieves, Barry Slate, Donna K. Teal, Tazmen Carlisle, Amy Kirtley-Hill, Kristy Parton, Debbie Shoffner, Cathy Edwards Simrell, Lynette Dickerson, Mark Rainey, Cathy Spangler Bruce

www.themailbox.com

©2004 by THE EDUCATION CENTER, INC.
All rights reserved.
ISBN# 1-56234-596-6

Manufactured in the United States
10 9 8 7 6 5 4 3 2

Contents

Eye-Catching Agenda Board

Here's a colorful way to let students know the daily schedule as they enter the classroom. Use colored chalk to draw a picture on the chalkboard that correlates with the current month or unit of study. Near the drawing, write the day's schedule along with any other important information, such as student birthdays or assignment due dates. Your students will no longer need to ask, "What are we going to do today?"

Rita Mohr
South Whitley Elementary
South Whitley, IN

A Show of Lights

Students waiting for the first school bell often become concerned when their teacher cannot be seen through a classroom window or door. To avoid these concerns, establish a signal for informing students that you are at school and just momentarily away from the classroom. For a simple and energy-efficient signal, burn only the center row of lights in your classroom. When students see this signal, they know that you are somewhere in the school.

Diane Scott, South Godwin Elementary, Grand Rapids, MI

Daily Schedule

Keep your youngsters abreast of each day's events by posting your daily schedule on a pocket chart. Write the numerals 1 through 12 on index cards; then position the cards in sequential order on the chart. Next, cut a supply of sentence strips in half and label each strip with the name of a different subject, class, or event that takes place on a recurring basis. To program the chart, position the labeled strips on the pocket chart in the order that they will occur. Store any unused strips nearby. At the end of each day, reprogram the chart to show the next day's schedule of events.

Tricia Peña, Acacia Elementary, Vail, AZ

Daily Schedule			
1	Opening	9	Lunch
2	Spelling	10	Math
3	Reading	11	Presentations
4	Group	12	Science
5	Art		
6	Recess		
7	Story		
8	P.E.		

Sign In, Please

Instantly put your youngsters' writing and thinking skills into gear with this morning routine. Attach a supply of charts such as the one shown to each of several clipboards. (You will need one clipboard per row, group, or table.) Before the youngsters arrive each morning, place each group's clipboard in a designated location. The first child to arrive in each group writes his name, his lunch plans, and his afterschool plans on the chart. He passes the chart to another student in his group. The completed charts are then passed to the teacher who calculates the daily lunch and attendance counts. The task of writing the daily information on a chart helps reinforces a student's thinking process, and it provides the teacher with valuable information.

Diane Bodnar, Jefferson Elementary, Bettendorf, IA

Name	Hot or Cold Lunch	Afterschool Plans
Deon	hot	go to scouts
Maria	hot	ride bus home

Papers for the Teacher

This timesaving tip helps the school day start smoothly! Rather than gathering assorted paperwork from students as you greet them each morning, ask youngsters to place the papers they have for you in a designated basket. Or go a step further and have them sort the paperwork into individual baskets labeled with specific categories, such as "Notes From Parents," "Homework," and "Permission Slips." Then, as time allows, address the paperwork in order of importance.

Barby Punzone, Public School 205, Brooklyn, NY

Good Morning!

Each morning do you find yourself reminding students to complete the same four or five tasks in order to prepare for the school day? Creating a class set of "Good Morning" cards may be just what you need! Design a card like the one shown that includes a good-morning message, a list of tasks, and a colorful sticker. Make a class set of cards; then use clear Con-Tact covering to attach one card to each child's desktop. These nifty reminders will help students get off to a great start each morning!

Nancy Lyde, Kiker Elementary School, Austin, TX

Good Morning and Welcome to a Great New Day!

Is your...
1. pencil sharpened?
2. homework ready to check?
3. snack at your desk?
4. heading on your paper?
5. warm-up paper ready?

Early Bird Tubs

Keep your early arrivals busy with these activity tubs. Gather several large storage tubs with lids. Put several of one type of item in each tub. For instance, put a variety of books in one tub and puzzles in another. Place each tub in a designated area of the room. As children arrive, invite them to play with the items in the tubs. To clean up, simply have children put the items back in the tubs and replace the lids. Periodically change the items in the tubs.

Dianne Giggey
Episcopal Day School, Pensacola, FL

Early Morning Management

End early morning confusion with this management system. Label each of three boxes with a different illustration to represent notes, papers, and lunch money. As youngsters enter the classroom each morning, they deposit their notes, papers, and labeled envelopes containing money in the appropriate boxes. With this system, you are free to greet youngsters first thing each morning and can take care of money and paperwork after youngsters are settled.

Sara Fakoury, Camden Elementary School, Camden, SC

Milk or Juice?

If your students get to choose a beverage for snacktime, try this idea to help make selections run like a charm. In advance, collect one clean half-pint carton for each of the following: white milk, chocolate milk, and juice. Cut the top off each carton. Mount each carton on a wall at students' eye level. Program each child's name on an individual craft stick, and place the sticks on a nearby shelf or table. Every morning as each child comes into the room, have him find his stick and place it in the beverage container of his choice. Using this timesaver, you'll be able to see at a glance your students' drink choices.

Brenda Wells And Donna Cook
Roseland Park Elementary, Picayune, MS

Name Recognition

Use this picture-perfect idea to take attendance and help your students recognize their names. Laminate a large school bus and school building tagboard cutout. Take a photograph of each child. Write his name on a photo-size piece of tagboard. Tape each child's name card to the back of his photo. Laminate the photos. Attach the hook side of a Velcro strip to the top of each side of the card. Then, for each photo, attach the loop side of a Velcro strip to the bus and the school cutout. To use, attach each photo to the bus cutout so that the name faces up. During group time, encourage each child to find his name and have him peek at the photo to check for correctness. Then have him remove the card and attach his photo to the school.

Lisa Lieb
Brooklyn Blue Feather Early Learning Center, New York, NY

Who's Not Here Today?

Here's a quick and simple way to take attendance each day. Write the word *girls* on one sentence strip and the word *boys* on another. Attach the strips to the side of a filing cabinet. Write each child's name on one side of a sentence strip. Attach pieces of magnetic tape to both sides of the sentence strip. Place each child's strip (name showing) on the cabinet under the appropriate heading. Request that each child turn his strip over each day as he arrives. You'll have a real-life math lesson each day as the class answers questions such as "How many boys are absent today?" and "Are there more girls or boys absent?"

Nancy Barad, Bet Yeladim Preschool, Columbia, MD

Taking Roll

To make taking attendance a simple matter and help youngsters practice name recognition, try this management aid. Personalize an apple cutout for each child. Attach a small piece of magnetic tape to the back of each cutout. On a wall, within your youngsters' reach, mount a strip of magnetic tape. Write each child's name on a small worm cutout and mount it above the strip of magnetic tape. Each morning, as each little one enters your room, have her locate her name on the worm and mount her apple on the magnetic tape below it. Change the cutouts to pumpkins and vines for October and turkeys and cornucopias for November. This quick and easy method will tell you at a glance which children are absent.

adapted from an idea by Becky Gibson
Ladonia Elementary, Auburn, AL

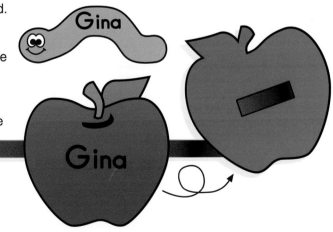

Attendance

Seasonal Nametags

To make taking attendance a simple matter and help youngsters practice name recognition, create durable seasonal nametags. For each child, personalize a laminated seasonal cutout such as a leaf, an apple, or a pumpkin. Attach a piece of magnetic tape to the back of each cutout. Then place these nametags on a table. Draw an illustration on the board to correspond with the nametags. For example, if the nametag is an apple cutout, draw a tree outline on the blackboard. Each morning, as each student enters your room, have him locate his nametag and mount it on the blackboard illustration. Change the nametags and the illustration monthly or seasonally. With this procedure you can see at a glance which children are absent, and youngsters will soon recognize their names and their classmates' names.

T. M. Hanak, Linden Little Rascals, Linden, MI

Look Who Popped In!

Attendance taking has new appeal with this "pop-ular" display. To begin, mount the title and a large bowl cutout on a board. Have each child cut out a large piece of construction paper popcorn and then write his name on it. Use pushpins to attach each popcorn piece to the board. As each child arrives, have him pin his popcorn piece above the bowl. With just a glance, you'll be able to tell who hasn't popped in for the day. If desired, provide some microwave popcorn and invite each child to have a few pieces after he records his attendance.

Lisa Cohen, Laurel Plains Elementary, New City, NY

Taking Attendance

To make taking roll a simple task, make an attendance display. To make this display, mount each child's photo on a construction paper rectangle and label the back with the child's name. Laminate it and then punch a hole at the top of each rectangle and attach a length of string. Attach the string to a bulletin board. Turn each rectangle to reveal the side showing the child's name. As each child arrives at school, have him locate his name and turn his picture over. Names still showing on the bulletin board will indicate at a glance who's not present.

Debbie Miller, Rockingham County Headstart, Eden, NC

Jared	Adriana	Jace	Gina	Jordan
😊	○	○	○	○
Cecilia	Nicholas	Matthew	Cohen	Thomas
○	○	😊	○	○
Gregory	Stephanie	Alexander	Amelia	Sonya
○	😊	○	😊	○
Patrick	Tyler	Austin		
○	○	😊	○	○

All Smiles

Taking attendance is a snap with this cheery chart! Visually divide a sheet of poster board to suit your needs and make a supply of happy face cutouts. Laminate the chart and cutouts. For easy reprogramming, tape name cards in place. Attach Velcro dots to the chart and to the backs of the cutouts. Display the chart and then store the cutouts in a container nearby. Each morning, a student adds a happy face to the chart to show that she's present. Each day before dismissal, a volunteer returns the cutouts to the container. If desired, supply special cutouts for students to use when they leave the room for bathroom breaks or special classes.

Kathleen Gillin, Cold Spring School, Doylestown, PA

Roll Call Responses

Add a little zip to your daily roll call! Instead of having youngsters respond with the usual, "Here," have them answer with words or phrases associated with the skills or themes they are studying. For example, during a dinosaur unit, students could respond with names of dinosaurs. Or, when youngsters are learning their personal information, they could respond with their phone numbers or addresses. Roll call is sure to take on a whole new meaning.

Patricia Montgomery, Fishburn Park Elementary, Roanoke, VA

Check-In

End early morning confusion with this easy management system. Personalize a library card pocket for each child and mount each pocket on a bulletin board. To make attendance cards, cut a supply of 3" x 5" construction paper cards from two contrasting colors. Pair contrasting cards, and glue them back-to-back. Label and simply illustrate one side of each card with the word "home" and the other side with "school." Insert a card in each pocket with the home side showing. As youngsters enter the classroom each morning, they check in by turning their cards to the school side. To check out in the afternoon, they turn their cards to the home side. With this system you can see at a glance who is absent.

Ann Rowe
Western Hills, Omaha Public Schools, Omaha, NE

Attendance

Attendance at a Glance

Here's a quick and interactive way to take attendance! Display a poster board chart, like the one shown, in an easily accessible location. Use a wipe-off marker to write a yes/no question on a laminated sentence strip; then mount the strip above the chart. Place a basket containing one personalized clothespin per student near the display. A student enters the room, reads the question (provide assistance as needed), and indicates her answer by clipping her clothespin on the appropriate side of the chart. A quick glance in the basket reveals which students are absent. At the end of the day, return all clothespins to the basket and reprogram the sentence strip with another yes/no question. Now that's a wonderful way to start the day!

Karen M. Moser
Wells Elementary, Plano, TX

"Egg-cellent" Attendance

Here's a springtime attendance-taking idea that involves students and also reinforces first- and last-name recognition. Gather a classroom supply of colorful plastic eggs. For each child, write her first name on one half of the egg and her last name on the other half. Place all of the halves in a basket. As a child enters your room, have her find her first name and her last name, connect the two pieces, and place the whole egg in a different basket (or an egg carton). During your group activities, ask a child to tell the class who is absent by looking at the remaining eggs.

Shannon Bass
Moore Haven Elementary School
Moore Haven, FL

Back-to-School Helpers

If you're approaching that overwhelming task of preparing your classroom for the beginning of school—help *could* be on the way! Simply ask a couple of particularly responsible older students (former students of yours) if they would be willing to donate a few hours to your cause. It's a real self-esteem booster for the students—and four extra hands for you!

Alvera Bade, Cedar School, Beatrice, NE

Meet the Teacher

Whether you hold your meet-the-teacher conferences at the end of one school year or the beginning of the next, this idea helps everybody make the most of them. When you schedule conferences, schedule two children and their parents for the same time. This way, in addition to meeting you, each child and his parent has the opportunity to meet another child and parent. Youngsters' first-day jitters are reduced—and so is your conference time!

Anita M. Ortiz, Red Sandstone Elementary, Vail, CO

All I Need To Know About Kindergarten

Please Return To School.

Thank you!

Entering Kindergarten Made Simple

Since kindergarten is sometimes the first school experience for children and parents (*as* parents!), use this idea to help organize the overwhelming odds and ends that can come with the start of school. For each child, label the outside of a two-pocket folder as shown. Add the child's name, your name, transportation informa-tion, and any other relevant information. Then gather your beginning-of-school paperwork, such as your welcome letter, a school handbook, and insurance forms. Indicate which of these papers must be returned to school by stamping them with a recognizable symbol, such as a star. (Be sure to write the code that you choose to use on the inside of the folder.) When you meet each parent, simply hand her a folder and encourage her to take it home and look over the information at her own pace. Then each child can use this folder to transport papers between home and school.

Beth Randall Davis, Lemira Elementary, Sumter, SC

Family Trees

Use this "tree-mendously" helpful display when first learning to recognize all your new students' parents and primary caregivers! On the first day of school or during open house, take a photograph of each student with her significant adults. Mount each photograph onto a tree cut-out; then label each tree with the family's name. Arrange the trees on a bulletin board titled "Our Family Trees." Your little ones will love looking at the display, and you will have a handy tool to help you quickly identify parents during those hectic first few days!

Sharon Davis, Lafayette Elementary, Oxford, MS

The Davis Tree

No More Jitters

Ease your youngsters' first-day anxieties with a cuddly class mascot! Introduce a stuffed animal to your class and pretend that he is whispering in your ear. Reassure him that school is a fun, safe place to be and that the children are friendly and kind. Explain to students that your friend is feeling shy and nervous about starting kindergarten. After students offer encouraging words and discuss their own concerns and fears, have your mascot guide them through each step of the day. It won't be long before your little ones feel relaxed and confident about school!

Jill Myers, Colstrip, MT

Lynn

Ms. Wellman's Class! Hop on in!

First-Week Themes

Help youngsters locate their classroom easily with a special color-coordinated theme for the first week of school. Meet with your kindergarten colleagues to determine a different color and related theme for each class. Prior to the first day of school, give or mail each parent a personalized shape nametag for his youngster to wear on the first day. Attach a trail of corresponding shapes onto the floor leading to your classroom door. On your door, mount a large character shape programmed to welcome your youngsters. The color-coded path and character make it easy for youngsters to find their classroom.

Cheryl Wellman, Quincy Head Start, Quincy, IL

Sticker Tags

Here a name! There a name! Where's *my* name? Use eye-catching stickers to help little ones find their own names on cubbies, tables, and coat hooks. For each child, collect multiple copies of a specific sticker design. As you prepare name labels for each child, attach the same sticker design to each of that child's name labels. This use of picture cuing will enable youngsters to find their own places and identify their names in no time at all.

Esther Gorelick, Yeshiva Zichron Moshe, South Fallsburg, NY

Magic Words

Ordinary words can work magic! At the beginning of the year, select a pair of words (such as *chocolate and vanilla* or *peanut butter and jelly*) and inform youngsters that these words will be the magic words. When you (or another adult) says the first magic word, youngsters turn to face you and then freeze and listen to your directions. When you're finished giving directions, say the second word. This word signals youngsters to resume working. Each time the class responds appropriately to the magic words, drop a token into a jar. When the jar is full, reward youngsters with a special treat. It's magic!

Pamela Green, Fishburn Park Elementary, Roanoke, VA

Dismissal Made Easy

Simplify dismissal during the first week of school with this organizational tip. In advance, prepare different sets of nametags to identify car riders, bus riders, walkers, and children attending after-school care. Estimate the number of children you will have in each category; then prepare that many blank nametags. As each new student arrives, have her attending adult write the child's name on the corresponding tag. Direct parents to return the tags to school with their child for the first week of school. A few minutes before dismissal, place each child's nametag around her neck; then group students by modes of transportation. Then, when the final bell rings, you can easily see how each of your little ones will get home.

Pam Shaffer
College Park Elementary, LaPorte, TX

Durable Nametags

For long-lasting nametags, try this nifty idea. Using the desired shape, die-cut a nametag for each student from a piece of craft foam. Use a permanent marker to write the student's name on the nametag; then punch a hole near the top of the tag with a hole puncher. Thread a length of ribbon through the hole and tie the ends of the ribbon together. These durable nametag necklaces can be used over and over again.

Judi Black, Beard Elementary, Fort Smith, AR

Movable Nametags

These convenient nametags help promote organization as well as add a decorative flair to your classroom. For each child, collect an empty, plastic yogurt container with a lid. To make a movable nametag, cover the container with decorative adhesive covering. Personalize a construction paper flower or seasonal cutout; then laminate it if desired. Tape the cutout to a pencil "stem"; then poke the pencil through the center of the lid on the container. Use these nametags to indicate seating or groupings, or to label freestanding artwork.

Kristy Curless
Walnut Creek Day School, Columbia, MO

Nifty Nametags

These easy-to-make clip-on nametags are versatile and durable! For each nametag you will need a plastic clip clothespin (with a hole in the handle) and a brass fastener. Personalize and laminate a poster board nametag for each youngster. Then punch a hole in the top of each nametag. Using brass fasteners, attach each nametag to a clothespin. To wear the nametag, students simply clip the clothespins to their clothing. It doesn't matter how the clothespin is clipped, since the nametag can rotate on the brass fastener.

Marlene Klukken
Blue Grass Elementary School, Knoxville, TN

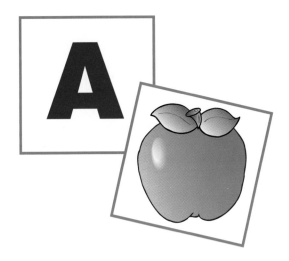

ABC Tickets

Try this novel idea for seating your youngsters during circle time. In advance, tape alphabet picture cards in a circle on the rug. Every morning as each student arrives, provide him with a letter card or "ticket" that corresponds with a picture card. Have each child locate his spot on the rug by matching the letter and picture cards. For a variation, have youngsters match either uppercase and lowercase letters or number words and numerals.

Jan McManus, Our Mother of Sorrows, Cincinnati, OH

Circle of Friends

Begin each day on a positive note with this daily sharing plan. Every morning gather students in a large circle. Beginning with the student to your left and proceeding clockwise, each child either shares an item or idea with his classmates in one or two sentences or he passes. Then ask the students to join hands and pass a silent hand squeeze around the circle. Lastly, deliver a positive thought for the day and dismiss the students to their desks. This sharing plan saves time, teaches students to summarize their thoughts, and creates a positive learning atmosphere.

Mary Beth Ghoreyeb
Brewster School, Durham, CT

Peaceful Puppet ✓

Use a peaceful critter to help curb classroom noise and signal to youngsters that circle time is about to begin. Give a designated puppet a name such as Bashful Bunny, Hush Puppy, or Quiet Koala. Explain to your youngsters that this critter will not come to circle time until everyone is quiet. Your little ones will be eager to hear what special message the critter whispers, so circle time is likely to get off to a peaceful start.

Ann Gudowski
Turtle Rock Private School, Lake Forest, CA

Circle Time

Circle-Time Surprise ✓ letter bag

If your circle time directly follows noon recess, you may find it difficult to settle your youngsters quickly and quietly. To ease this transition, decorate a large, covered basket with a bow and/or a mylar helium balloon. Each day secretly place any items in the basket that are needed for that day's activity (for example, a puppet and a book, or objects needed to play a game). Wait until students are quietly settled for circle time before revealing the basket's contents.

Sandy Greensfelder
Naples Elementary, Naples, Italy

Sharing Strips

Make the most of show-and-tell with this simple management system. Personalize a library pocket for each student; then attach the pockets to a sheet of poster board. Each student begins the week with a construction paper sharing strip in his pocket. Students are invited to share one object per week. (They may share with their voices each day.) When a student chooses to share an object, he retrieves his sharing strip and hands it to the teacher before he begins. By using this simple sharing plan, students are encouraged to share events rather than toys and other material items.

JoAnn Prehn, Sugar Creek Elementary School, Verona, WI

Sharing Sessions

Just in time—a great idea for managing student sharing sessions! Each day set aside time for a predetermined number of students to share their "egg-citing" news during circle time. Display an hourglass egg timer; then, as each student starts to share his news with the class, invert the timer. If the sand in the timer runs out before the youngster is finished, inform him that his sharing time is over and ask him to wrap up his story. Before you know it, students will be summarizing their stories so that they can make the most of their sharing sessions.

Judith Casey
Chatham School District
Chatham, NJ

Classroom Jobs and Helpers

A Special Teddy Bear

Here's a warm and fuzzy way to display your helper's name each day. For each child, personalize a construction paper heart cutout and punch a hole in each cutout. Every morning, select one child to be the helper of the day. Then thread the corresponding cutout onto a length of yarn. Tie the yarn around a teddy bear's neck and display this fuzzy friend on your desk. Your little ones will be anxious to see who the helper is each day.

Laurie Matt
Christ the King School, Overland Park, KS

Super Person

Here's a great way to choose your daily classroom helper. Display an apple cutout in your room labeled "Super Person." Also ask each child to bring a recent photograph of himself to school. Stack the photographs in a desk drawer. Each morning attach the top photograph (in the stack) to the cutout. The featured child becomes the classroom helper for the day and is responsible for performing tasks such as running errands and distributing papers. At the end of the day, remove the photograph from the cutout and place it at the bottom of the photograph stack. Simple and efficient!

Lee Nelson, Rural Point Elementary, Mechanicsville, VA

Leader for the Day

Try this fun alternative to a weekly helper display! Create a fabric or felt chair cover like the one shown (be sure to label both sides). Each day select a classroom leader by slipping the cover over the back of a student's chair. The classroom leader becomes the line leader, paper passer, messenger, and all-around teacher's assistant for the day. At the end of the day, transfer the chair cover to the back of another student's chair. If desired, select the leaders in alphabetical order. Each student will eagerly anticipate her turn as classroom leader, and you'll be boosting self-esteems *and* reinforcing alphabetizing skills!

Margarett Mendenhall
Mary Feeser Elementary School, Elkhart, IN

Classroom Jobs and Helpers

Helping Hands

If you cluster your students' desks, here's a handy way to designate weekly group helpers. Attach a colorful hand cutout (laminated for durability) to the back of one chair in each group. This child becomes his group's helper for the week. His responsibilities might include distributing and collecting papers, student folders, and math manipulatives, and keeping his group's area neat and tidy. After one week, transfer each cutout to a different group member's chair. Continue in this manner until each group member has been a helper; then repeat the rotation.

Nicole Lomax
Smiths Primary, Smiths, AL

Calendar

Eva

Matthew

Adam

Helpful Helpers Chart

Keeping up with the helpers of the day or week can be a job in itself! So try this method. Program each of your classroom jobs on a different vertical strip of tagboard. On each strip, below the job title, list (in random order) each student in the class. Using a different color of paper clip or clothespin for each strip, assign the helper for each job by clipping a paper clip next to that child's name. When it is time to change helpers, simply move each paper clip to the next child's name.

Laurie Rickel
New Hope Christian School, Circleville, OH

Classroom Jobs and Helpers

Job Gallery

Your youngsters can remember their daily job assignments with the help of this picture job chart. Take photographs of items that represent each of the jobs assigned to your students. For example, you may photograph a broom to represent the job of sweeping, an aquarium for pet care, or a trash can for emptying the trash. Attach the pictures to a low bulletin board so the children can easily see them. Place the name of the student responsible for each job under the picture for that job. Throughout the day, the children can check the job chart to remind themselves of their jobs. It's a picture-perfect way to promote independence and responsibility.

Jan McManus, Our Mother of Sorrows, Cincinnati, OH

Helper of the Day

If you have difficulty keeping your classroom helper chart current due to frequent changes in your student enrollment, consider this idea. List your students' names in a column at one end of a magnetic chalkboard. Each day position a colorful magnet alongside the helper of the day. For convenience, begin with the name at the top of the list and move the magnet downwards, one name per day. Students' names can easily be added to or deleted from the list.

LuEtta Culp, Louis B. Russell #48, Indianapolis, IN

Helping Hands

This personalized helpers' chart will display a spectrum of colorful helpers. To make a chart, cut approximately eight-inch-wide strips of tagboard. About two inches above the bottom of the long edge of each tagboard strip, write students' names in colors according to the order of the rainbow: red, orange, yellow, green, blue, and violet. Have each child make a handprint above her name, matching the color of paint for the handprint to the color used to write her name (or using the paint color of her choice). Once they're dry, hang the strips in a row across the top of a chalkboard.

Draw a picture for each job assignment (such as a milk carton for the milk helper). Laminate these pictures; then attach a clothespin upside down to the top back of each picture. Hang each picture under a different child's name. By moving the pictures to the right each day, you'll have the opportunity to reinforce left-to-right movement for reading readiness. Once a picture has been moved completely down the line of names, be sure to move it back to the beginning to start again. At the end of the year, cut the handprints apart and send them home as thank-yous to your happy helpers.

Peggy Bierma
Calvin Christian School
Edina, MN

Homework Tracker

Add a Collection Officer to your job chart, and you'll find it's a breeze to keep up with homework assignments. At the start of each day, have your Collection Officer gather the previous day's homework assignment. If a student neglected to do his homework, the Collection Officer has the student sign a dated card. You can quickly examine the card to see whose homework is missing. These dated cards are also easy to store for future reference, like during conference and report card times.

Shannon Reinighaus, Lowry Elementary, Tampa, FL

March 12, 2004
Ricky Tyler
Lisa

Manipulatives Coordinator

Save time by enlisting your students' help in organizing classroom manipulatives for quick and easy distribution. Every Monday assign a student to be the Manipulative Coordinator, or M.C., for the week. Each morning have the M.C. count and sort the manipulatives needed for that day. You can count on plenty of student interest in this official-sounding job.

Kim Lehmker, Our Shepherd Lutheran School, Birmingham, MI

Directions Director

Use this idea to encourage students to listen carefully to oral directions. Each week appoint a student helper to be the Directions Director. Explain that it is the responsibility of this student to carefully listen to and remember your oral instructions. Any students who did not listen carefully must ask the Directions Director for assistance. Not only will you be free to help students in other ways, but your youngsters' listening skills are bound to improve!

Sherry Kay, Fox Prairie Elementary, Stoughton, WI

Feed the Pig

This little pig is perfect for motivating your little ones to pitch in and clean up! To make one, use a utility knife to cut an opening opposite the handle of a clean bleach bottle to represent the pig's mouth as shown. Use masking tape to cover the edges of the opening. Next, paint the bottle pink. When the paint is dry, add eyes, felt ears, a pipe cleaner tail, and spools for feet. During cleanup time, you will hear lots of delightful squeals as one student carries the pig around so that others can pick up bits of scrap to feed the hungry paper-eater!

Karen Saner
Burns Elementary, Burns, KS

Cleanup Call

Keep your students focused on the task of cleaning up with this cute call-and-response song. Signal cleanup time by singing the first line of the song. Continue singing until the room is clean and you're ready for your next activity.

Clean Up
(sung to the tune of "The Banana Boat Song")

Teacher: Clean up!
Students: Clee-ee-ee-ee-ean up!
Teacher: Clean up your space and check out the floor!
Students: Clean up our space and check out the floor!
         Clean up our space and check out the floor!

Deb Scala, Mt. Tabor Elementary, Mt. Tabor, NJ

Responsibility Chart

To guarantee that everyone participates during cleanup time, use a responsibility chart. Cut out catalog pictures of the various types of toys, games, and manipulatives that are used in your classroom. Glue these pictures to a sheet or two of tagboard, and label each picture. Laminate the chart. Write each child's name on a self-sticking note and post it next to the job for which he will be responsible. At cleanup time, your happy helpers need only to glance at the chart to see which areas they are to clean up. Periodically change job responsibilities by moving the self-sticking notes.

Coreen VanDerWoude
Rochester Christian School, Rochester, NY

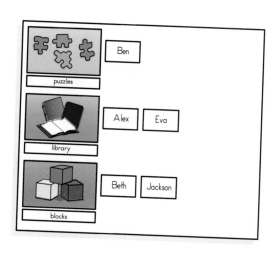

Clever Cleanup

If you need help keeping your classroom tidy, enlist the help of litter-eating Egabrag (*garbage* spelled backwards). Cut the shape of a dust ball from gray construction paper; then add facial features and the message "Please feed Egabrag!" Use clear Con-Tact covering to attach the cutout to your classroom trash can. When you start to see signs of classroom litter, a gentle reminder such as, "Did I just hear Egabrag's tummy growl?" will have students cleaning up in no time!

Jo Fryer
Kildeer Countryside School, Long Grove, IL

Icky-Sticky Cleanup

Cleanup motivation is no problem at all when you use this sticky little tip! If an area of your room is littered with tiny paper scraps, glitter, or other small art supplies, loosely wrap the hand of your helper(s) in masking tape—with the sticky side out. To clean up, the child repeatedly touches his wrapped hand to the littered area. For variety, try wrapping your cleanup helper's shoe in the same manner. After a little walk around the room, cleanup is all wrapped up!

Heather Peachey, Bowman School Extended Day Program, Lexington, MA

Color-Coded Cleanup

Here's a colorful way to share the cleaning responsibilities in your classroom—and reinforce reading! Divide your class into five groups. Choosing a different color of construction paper for each group, make a nametag for each child in the group. Using white construction paper, make a card for each day of the week. Mount the names (in color groups) on a bulletin board or wall. Each day, mount the corresponding day-of-the-week card above one of the cleanup groups. A quick glance will tell your children who is responsible for cleanup.

Mark Pittelkow
Jewish Community Center
  of the Greater St. Paul Area
St. Paul, MN

Tuesday				
David	Courtney	Todd	Phoebe	Monica
Jenny	Tyler	Sarah	Chandler	Joey
Melinda	Shanda	Kevin	Ross	Marcel
Peter	Teesha	Cathy	Rachel	Bill

Trash Boxes

For an easy solution to messy tables, try this neat idea. Cut off the top portion from a small detergent box with a handle. Use Con-Tact covering to cover the box. Place one box on each table. Throughout the day, have youngsters discard paper scraps and trash in the box. At the end of the day, designate one child from each table to empty the box. Now that's a sure way to keep your room spotless!

Terri Mack, Oaks Road Elementary, New Bern, NC

The Cleanup Train

When your classroom needs a little extra straightening up, announce that it's time for the Cleanup Train. Ask each child to line up behind you and hold on to the waist of the person in front of her. Begin quietly chugging around the room. As you see an area that needs attention, call out (for example), "First stop, block center." Then the first child behind you steps off the train and begins to clean up the block center. Meanwhile the train continues quietly chugging along, calling out stops such as "Second stop, art area" and "Third stop, trash can." Each time a stop is announced, the child directly behind you steps off the train to tend to that stop. When a child's work is done in a particular area, she rejoins the train at the end of the line. When your room is in order, you say, "Last stop!" and the whole class joins you in a round of "Toot! Toot!"

Chava Shapiro, Beth Rochel School, Monsey, NY

Visits From the Desk Fairy

Promote reading as you motivate students to keep neat-as-a-pin desks! Create a supply of duplicated notes from the Desk Fairy similar to the ones shown. Attach a small sticker or another treat to each one. When the students are out of the room, slip a note from the Desk Fairy into each neatly organized student desk. Once the word gets out, youngsters will eagerly keep tidy desks in anticipation of the Desk Fairy's next visit!

Bonnie Lanterman
Armstrong Elementary School
Hazelwood, MO

This is a neat desk to hide out in during the day. From the Desk Fairy

I can skate in circles in this neat and clean desk! From the Desk Fairy

Wow, you sure do keep your desk neat and clean! From the Desk Fairy

I am hiding behind all your neat things. From the Desk Fairy

Cleanup

The Inspector's Coming!

If you have a set of classroom walkie-talkies, classroom cleanup has just taken on new ease! When it's time to clean up, assign one student to be the inspector. Have the inspector check all areas of the classroom. Encourage him to radio in any spots that might need extra attention. A chance to be the inspector is enough to motivate almost anyone to participate in classroom cleanup!

DeAnna Martin
Hargett Elementary
Irvine, KY

Cleanup Party!

Do your classroom tables need a good cleaning? If so, throw a party! All you need is some non-mentholated shaving cream and about 20 pairs of little hands. First clear off your tables and invite each child to have a seat. Squirt out some shaving cream in front of each child; then encourage him to fingerpaint with the cream—swirling, twirling, and whirling it about. When the artistry subsides, have each child rinse his hands as you wipe off each table with a damp sponge. Your tables will be clean and your room will carry a clean, fresh scent!

Maddalena E. McKee, Trinity Regional School, Northport, NY

Cleanup Snakes!

Cleanup will be a "sssnap" when using cleanup snakes. To make a cleanup snake, decorate an old tube sock to resemble a snake. Keep a quantity of these critters in a basket so students will have easy access to them. When it's time to clean up a dirty tabletop, shelf, or floor, have a youngster put a cleanup snake on his hand and slither away to wipe up the mess.

Evelyn Moses
Raleigh Christian Academy
Durham, NC

Tickets, Please

Promote a clean classroom with this "quicker-picker-upper." Just before your youngsters line up to leave the classroom, announce that they will need tickets in order to leave the room. A ticket is a given number of scraps of paper (or whatever is necessary to clean the room). Wait by the door with a wastebasket as each child deposits her ticket before leaving. The children love the idea and the room gets cleaned. Now that's the ticket!

Debbie Palmer
A New Beginning Christian School
Cleveland, GA

Catnap Cleanup

Follow these steps to make classroom cleanup a quiet game. While you pretend to be a sleeping cat, have your students pretend to be mice. Explain that as the cat naps, the mice will clean up the classroom as quietly as possible to avoid waking up the cat. Ham up your role by snoring loudly. "Wake up" with an exaggerated stretch and yawn to give your little mice time to scurry to their desks. You'll find that your classroom has been cleaned up with a minimal amount of fuss and noise—except for your snoring, of course!

Mary Sue Owens, Bassetti Elementary, Abilene, TX

Litter Jugs

If you want a solution for messy tables, then try this neat tip. Cut off the top portion of a one-gallon milk jug (keeping the handle intact). Place one milk jug on each table. Throughout the day, have youngsters discard paper scraps and trash in the jug. At the end of each day, designate one child from each table to empty the jug. This is a sure way to keep cleanup simple and your room spotless.

Sharon Walker
Danville Elementary
Danville, AL

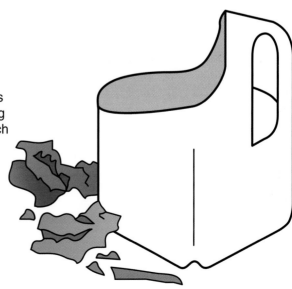

Cleanup

Wonderful Wipes

This tip makes classroom cleanup a breeze! In a note to parents, request that each student bring a container of baby wipes to school. Leave one container in a location that is easily accessible to students and store the rest of the containers for later use. You and your students will discover that baby wipes are especially handy for cleaning desktops, tabletops, chalk ledges, overhead transparencies, and sticky hands. As an added bonus, you'll have the freshest-smelling room around!

Laura Peter, Our Lady of the Rosary, Cincinnati, OH

Grab That Garbage!

This cleanup game leaves your room looking tidy at the end of the day. Prior to game time, survey the floor and secretly identify one paper scrap (or other item destined for the trash can) as the piece for the day. To play the game, students quickly gather garbage from the floor for approximately one minute. The students then return to their desks and display the garbage they have collected. The student who collected the mystery piece wins a sticker. All of the garbage is then deposited in a trash can.

Brenda Britton
Washington Elementary School, Noblesville, IN

The Silent Approach

Ever wonder why it's such a challenge to get students to quickly and quietly clean up the classroom? Perhaps a new approach will help! When it's time to clean up, say, "One for the money. Two for the show." Then have the rest of the class join in on, "Three for silent cleanup. Go, class, go!" With this cue as a prompt, students silently and cooperatively make quick work of the cleaning to be done.

Tina McSoley
Warfield Elementary School
Indiantown, FL

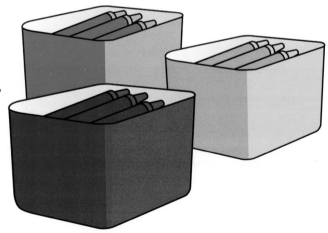

Cleanup Song

Your room will sparkle at cleanup time when you use a decorated wand called Mr. Twinkle. Glue a tagboard star cutout to the end of a 12-inch wooden dowel. Then, when it's time to clean up, lightly tap each youngster on the shoulder with Mr. Twinkle as you sing this song:

(sung to the tune of "Twinkle, Twinkle, Little Star")

Twinkle, twinkle, little star,
Time to clean up where you are.
Put each toy back in its place.
Keep a smile on your face.
Twinkle, twinkle, little star,
Time to clean up where you are.

Jeanne Taylor, YMCA Preschool, Thornton, CO

Class Cleanup

During the last few minutes of each day, have students complete small jobs in your classroom. Allow youngsters who have quickly prepared for dismissal to do jobs such as picking up paper scraps, erasing the chalkboard, and straightening the bookshelves. Your students will be motivated to promptly gather their belongings in order to take part in your class cleanup.

Mary Dinneen, Mountain View School, Bristol, CT

Musical Cleanup

Spruce up your classroom in no time with this upbeat game. During cleanup time, play a lively record or tape. Periodically stop the music and have students "freeze." After a few seconds, resume the music and have students continue the cleanup. This musical twist adds fun to an often tiresome task, and the results will be dazzling!

Kim Schultze, Olney Elementary, Olney, MD

Cleanup

Water at Your Fingertips

If you're without a sink in your room and want to eliminate youngsters' unnecessary trips to the restroom sink, then try this helpful hint. In advance, fill a spray bottle with water. Keep it nearby throughout the day and spritz the water to clean up spills, messy fingers, and tables.

Dianne Giggey, Episcopal Day School, Pensacola, FL

Rub-a-dub-dub!

This sweet-smelling idea will keep little fingers fresh and clean. Collect scraps of various scented soaps. Cut one nylon leg from a pair of pantyhose. Place the soap scraps in the pantyhose leg; then tie it to your classroom water faucet. When your little ones need to wash their hands, they simply rub their wet hands on the soap bag. Neat and clean!

Maria Cuellar Munson
Unity Caring Club, Dallas, TX

Super Soapers

Too much soap? Too little soap? No soap at all? Send Super Soapers to the rescue! Using a regular pump-soap dispenser, squirt a dab of soap into each child's hand as he lines up to wash his hands. As youngsters learn to recognize what an appropriate amount of soap is, begin asking for volunteers to be the Super Soaper of the day. This simple procedure saves soap, yet ensures that everyone has clean, washed hands.

Kathy Martin
Nellie Reed Elementary, Vernon, MI

Three Minutes

During the last few minutes of each day, enlist the help of your students with this timely cleanup tip. Choose a cleanup helper to set and monitor a timer for three minutes. Challenge your youngsters to quietly clean up before the sand slips through the timer or the bell on the timer rings. Have your cleanup helper alert your students when time is about to expire. With this quick and easy method, your room will be spotless in a matter of minutes.

Pat Bollinger
Leopold R-3
Leopold, MO

Snacktime Tip

Plastic bowls make snacktime cleanup quick and easy! Before serving snacks, place a large plastic bowl in the center of each table. After each youngster finishes his snack, ask him to place his trash in the bowl. Then have helpers empty the bowls into the trash can and wipe them out. Cleanup is a snap!

Sheila Weinberg, Warren Point School, Fair Lawn, NJ

Dismissal

Chair Mailboxes

Individual chair mailboxes put an end to paper clutter. To make a chair mailbox, cut the top off a cereal box; then cut away portions of the sides and front as shown. Cover the box with Con-Tact paper and personalize it if desired. Punch two holes near the top of the box back. Thread a length of yarn through the holes and tie it to the back of a youngster's chair. Throughout the day, place notes, letters, art projects, or other papers for youngsters to take home in their mailboxes. At the end of the day, have each youngster check her mailbox, remove the papers, and take them home.

Roxanne Rast

Neatness Counts

Tidy desks are the norm when daily desk checks become part of your routine. A few minutes before end-of-the-day dismissal, announce the impending desk check. When a child has straightened the inside of his desk and has tidied the floor space around it, he stands and waits quietly. A quick nod or verbal okay indicates to a child that he may gather his belongings and wait quietly in a designated location for dismissal. Since a clean desk is the ticket to dismissal, students quickly learn that keeping their areas neat throughout the day leaves less tidying to do at the day's end.

Ruth Watson, Field Elementary School, Littleton, CO

Dismissal Reminders

Here's an easy reminder for when a parent sends a note saying that his child is going home on a different bus or being picked up after school. Post these notes near your classroom door where children line up to go home. As children prepare to leave, you"ll see at a glance who has made special dismissal arrangements.

Marlene Kimmell
Graysville Elementary School, Graysville, IN

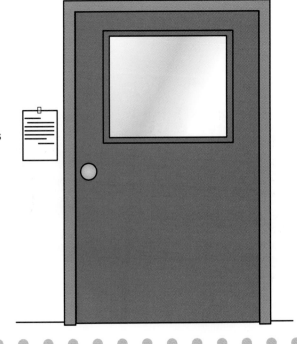

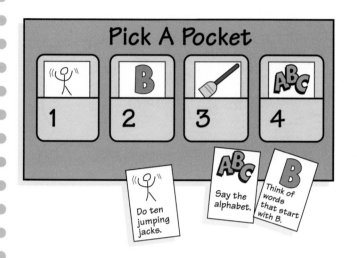

Pick a Pocket ✓

Caught with just a spare minute or two? Here's the perfect spare-minute filler for review! Glue ten to 20 library pockets on a sheet of poster board; then number each pocket. For each pocket, write a review activity on a blank index card (trimmed, if necessary, to fit the pocket). Slide a card into each pocket. When you have a spare minute to fill, ask a child to pick a pocket. Then have the class do the activity on that card. To add to the learning, turn the card over before replacing it in the pocket. Then have youngsters count how many cards have been chosen and how many are left, guiding them to make *more* and *less* statements. Change the activities on the cards as needed.

Debbie Reed, Satilla Elementary, Douglas, GA

Five-Minute Filler

Need a time filler for those extra minutes during the day? Keep the ball rolling in your classroom with this skill-reinforcement idea. Seat your youngsters in a circle. Roll a sponge ball to a student. Then ask him a review question about the first letter of his name, the beginning sound of a word, or the color of an object. Continue in this manner by rolling the ball to another student. This fun-filled activity is certain to keep everyone on the ball.

Lynn Cadogan
Starkey Elementary, Seminole, FL

Make Every Minute Count ✓

Keep five-minute fillers at your fingertips with this handy storage tip! Photocopy and cut out your favorite time-filler activities; then mount them onto individual index cards. Hole-punch the cards and bind them on a large metal or plastic ring. Continue adding to the collection as desired. The next time you have a few minutes between activities, reach for your ring of favorite time fillers. Your spare minutes quickly become teachable moments!

Donna Gregory
Hodge Elementary
Denton, TX

Line Up and Go

Lineup Chant

Prepare your youngsters for a quiet classroom exit by having them recite a short chant each time they line up. By the time the chant is finished, students will be ready to make a silent entry into the hall.

Carolyn Kanoy, Old Town Elementary
Winston-Salem, NC

*I'm giving myself a great big hug.
I'm standing straight and tall.
I'm looking right ahead of me.
I'm ready for the hall.*

Choo Choo Chant

This little chant works wonders to help your children concentrate on forming and *staying in* a line. After practicing the art of lining up, introduce this chant to help with the task at hand.

Our line needs a leader,
And it needs a caboose.
We'll make our line straight,
And we'll keep our line loose.

No pushing, no shoving,
Our hands at our sides,
As we walk, walk, walk,
In our line.

Sandra Steele
Jefferson School, Princeton, IL

Sing-Along Lineup

To encourage students to line up quickly and quietly, begin singing a song that your students know. Invite students to sing along as they take their places in line. Continue singing until students are organized and ready to go. Lining up has never been more fun!

Debbie Byrne
Candor Elementary School, Candor, NY

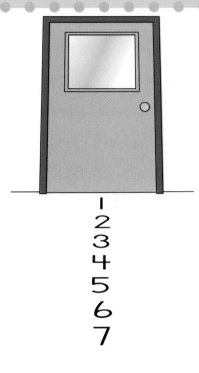

1
2
3
4
5
6
7

Number Lineup

Teach number recognition and ordinal positions as your students line up. Attach vinyl, adhesive-backed numbers (available from office supply stores) in sequence on the floor. When you're ready for youngsters to line up, call on a child to stand on the first number. Have him name a child to stand on the next number. Continue in this manner until all the children are in line. Encourage little ones to name the numbers and to use words to describe their ordinal positions such as *first, second,* and *third.*

Joan M. Richardson
Feldkirchner Elementary School, Green Brook, NJ

Alphabetical Lineup ✓

Get students in line quickly with this method. Label a set of 26 index cards with capital or lowercase letters. Ask each child to select a labeled card. Then call out each letter in order. As a letter is called, the child holding that card lines up. This method stops the mad rush for the front of the line and reinforces letter recognition as well. *A, B, C, D, E, F, G.* Will you please line up with me?

Laura Bentley
Ramsay-Victoria School, Calgary, Alberta, Canada

Letter-Perfect Lineup ✓

Try this letter-perfect lineup tip! Program a class supply of clothespins with the letters of the alphabet (add selected blends or digraphs if you have more than 26 students). Every Monday dispense the clothespins, making sure the line leader for the week receives clothespin A. During the week, students line up alphabetically by their assigned letters. The following Monday, collect and redistribute the clothespins. It's as easy as A, B, C!

Christine Schirmer
Van Zant Elementary School, Marlton, NJ

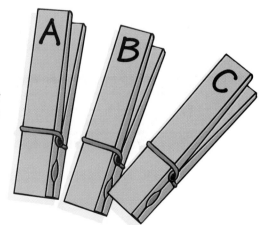

Line Up and Go

I've Got a Secret

Motivate your students to wait quietly with this top-secret activity. Whisper a secret message to the first person in line. Ask this student to whisper the message to the second person in line, who whispers it to the third student. When the message reaches the last student in line, ask him to say the secret aloud. Restate the original secret, and have the students compare the two versions. By this time your wait will be over, leaving your students to wonder how time passed so quickly!

Beth Martin
Dr. Brown Elementary, Waldorf, MD

Phone-Number Reinforcement

Here's a "phone-tastic" way to practice telephone-number recognition. For each student, program a wooden craft stick with her name and telephone number. Then, when you want to select a student to answer a question or to line up, call out her telephone number instead of her name. "555-0161, you may line up first."

Patricia Wilson
Wheatland Elementary, Elsie, NE

Links for Lining Up

Motivate students to line up quickly and quietly with this paper-chain incentive. Keep a supply of construction paper strips and a stapler on hand. To begin, tape one link of a paper chain to the top of the door frame. Explain to your students that each time they line up satisfactorily they will earn an additional link on the chain. When the paper chain extends to a predetermined length, reward the students with a special treat or privilege. Continue offering added incentives as the length of the chain increases.

Jennifer Ursta and Sandra Loudon
Claude Huyck School
Kansas City, KS

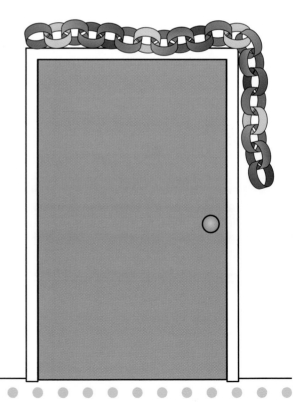

Stop Sign Lineup

When your students line up for lunch or recess, do they know where you want them to stand? Designate the place for students to line up with a stop sign. Cut the stop sign from red poster board. Write the word STOP on the cutout and tape it to the floor where you want the line leader to stand. Have the other children line up behind him.

Kim Williamson
East End Elementary School
Selma, AL

Daily Lineup

Keep students lining up in an orderly fashion day after day! Arrange the students' desks in five groups and name each group for a different weekday. A group lines up first during its namesake day. The first group is followed in line by the group named for the next weekday, and then the next, and so on until all groups are in line. With this systematic approach, lining up quickly and quietly soon becomes a habit!

Pat Hart, C. A. Henning School, Troy, IL

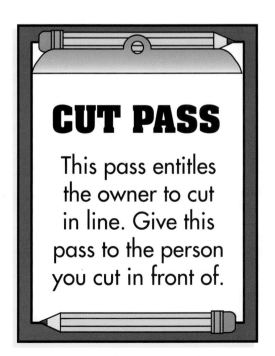

CUT PASS

This pass entitles the owner to cut in line. Give this pass to the person you cut in front of.

Cut Passes

Use this idea to minimize problems when students are lining up to leave the room. At the beginning of the year, give each child a cut pass like the one shown. If a child wants to cut in line so that he can stand near a friend, he forfeits his pass to the person he cut in front of. Since children rarely want to give up their cut passes, this idea works like a charm.

Mardi Dilks
Cooper City Elementary
Cooper City, FL

Line Up and Go

Noise Control Game ✓

Employ the domino effect to quiet classroom chatter before your students exit the room. Have the first student in line put his index finger to his lips and turn to the person behind him, showing this quiet signal. Then the second student in line puts his index finger to his lips and turns to the person behind him to show him the same quiet signal. In turn, each student continues the domino effect of the quiet signal until it reaches the last child in line. You won't even hear a whisper with this quiet chain reaction.

Sandy Simko
Brecht Elementary School
Lancaster, PA

Marshmallow Shoes

Before venturing out into the school hallways, have your youngsters put on imaginary marshmallow shoes. Explain to students that noisy feet can disturb other students who are hard at work. Because marshmallows are soft and noiseless, shoes having marshmallow soles are perfect for wearing when quiet walking is needed. Don't be surprised to find your students slipping off their humdrum footwear and opting for their imaginary shoes, even without your asking!

Judith Casey, Chatham School District, Chatham, NJ

The Magic Door ✓

Keep hallway chatter down to a minimum with this magical idea. Tell your students to pretend that the doorway from your classroom to the hall is magic and when you step through it, you lose your voice. Model this behavior by moving your lips but not speaking. You'll be amazed just how quiet the hallways are once your youngsters are under the spell of the magical doorway.

Marci Reimer-Haber
Ross Elementary School, Nashville, TN

Hallway Manners

Here's an upbeat way to quickly settle your troop before leading it into the hallway. When the class is lined up, sing each line of the cadence call shown, pausing for students to repeat each line after you. This military-style chant readies your brigade to march through the hall with pride!

Amy Kallelis
Cold Spring Elementary
Doylestown, PA

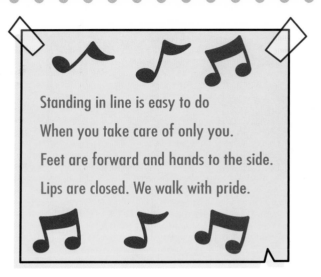

Standing in line is easy to do

When you take care of only you.

Feet are forward and hands to the side.

Lips are closed. We walk with pride.

Hallway Management

An imaginary high wire may prove successful in transporting students quickly and quietly through school hallways. When traveling from one location to another, have students pretend they are tightrope walkers. Whether students are following a line in the linoleum or an imaginary high wire, their intense concentration makes for a surprisingly quiet hallway journey!

Brooke A. Bock
Warriors Mark Elementary, Tyrone, PA

Walk Along

Skill recognition happens to be a nice fringe benefit that comes with this method of crowd control. In advance post numbers (or shapes, animals, or letters) at varying intervals along commonly walked paths in your school (for example, to the cafeteria). As your class moves in a line from place to place, instruct the line leader to go to the [two] and stop. This enables the line to move on within limits, while you are freed up to do whatever crowd control is needed at the middle or back of the line.

Nancy Nason Biddinger

Lunch and Snacks

Keep the Change

If your youngsters sometimes lose their lunch or snack money, then try this efficient way to store it. In advance, purchase a hardware storage unit containing lots of miniature drawers. Personalize the outside of each drawer with a different student's name. Each morning as students enter the room, have each child place his lunch and/or snack money in his drawer. No more lost coins!

Brenda Wells and Donna Cook

Money Manager

Are you looking for individual containers for children's lunch or milk money? M&M's mini candy containers work great! Remove the label from each tube; then use a permanent marker to write a child's name on each tube. These containers will accommodate coins up to a quarter's size and rolled dollar bills. As far as emptying the candy from the tubes in the first place? No problem there!

Brenda Harris
Montana Vista Primary, El Paso, TX

Reward-Winning Restaurant

When you're ready to reward hardworking or well-behaved students, invite them out to lunch! Don't worry; you won't have to go far to find a suitable restaurant. Your own classroom will do nicely. On the day of the special lunch, decorate a table with a fancy tablecloth and a centerpiece. Play soft background music and provide dessert if desired. Students will enjoy eating their lunches in style. Who knows? You might even earn a four-star rating for your charming classroom cafe.

Marilyn Cameron
Gray Elementary, Houston, TX

Taking Turns

To make sure youngsters have equal opportunities to use playground equipment such as rubber balls and jump ropes, put this idea into action. Label each piece of equipment; then label class rosters to match. As children use the equipment, have them cross off their names on the appropriate class rosters. When all of the names have been crossed off a list, post a new roster.

Mary Dinneen
Mountain View School, Bristol, CT

Jump Rope With Red Handles
Seth Goodman
~~Katie O'Neil~~
Charles Bruce
Maria Garcia
~~Henry James~~
Becca Clay
~~Derrick Watkins~~

Outside Organization

Make outside play run like a charm with these helpful hints. Review safety rules before going outside, and have your youngsters use the restrooms and get a drink. Fill a milk crate or cardboard box with items that may be needed while you're outdoors (such as tissues, wet wipes, rubber gloves, a first-aid kit, a garbage bag, and small outside games such as bubbles, jacks, and chalk). Replace any items as you use them and you're ready for next time!

Joy Morey
Walnut Grove Little House
West Mifflin, PA

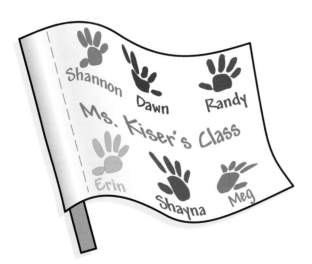

Flag 'em In

Here's a high-flying alternative to blowing a whistle at the end of recess: Wave a special class flag! As each student notices the flag, she tells another child until all are lined up and ready to go. Add motivation to this process by allowing the first child to arrive to hold the flag. For more flag-watching incentive, have students help create the class flag by using fabric paint to make student handprints on a sheet of fabric. Sew a pocket narrow enough to securely hold a dowel in place; then slip the cloth over the dowel. Betsy Ross would be impressed!

Cheryl Kiser
Jackson Elementary, Boise, ID

Transitions and Attention-Getters

Time for Fishing

When your class has a spare minute or two, the time is right for fishing! In advance, write a different transition activity on each of a supply of fish cutouts. (For volunteers or substitutes, write a description of each activity on the back of each cutout.) Slide a metal paper clip onto each fish; then store all the fish in a fishbowl. Make a fishing pole by tying one end of a string around a magnet and the other end around a wooden dowel. When you need a filler activity, you or a child can fish for an activity from your school of fish.

Anita Lieberman
Beth Sholom Goldman Nursery School, Elkins Park, PA

Transition Tune

Get students to tune in when it's time to change activities with this catchy song.

(sung to the tune of "Frère Jacques")

Are you listening? Are you listening?	*Teacher sings.*
Yes, I am! Yes, I am!	*Children sing.*
Now it's time to [clean up].	*Teacher sings.*
Now it's time to [clean up].	*Children sing.*
Here we go!	*Teacher sings.*
Here we go!	*Children sing.*

Repeat the song, substituting *line up, eat lunch,* and *go home* for the underlined phrase.

adapted from an idea by Garla Morin, Pretty Eagle Catholic School, Hardin, MT

Hands-On Attention Getter

You'll have all eyes on you when all hands are involved. If you study one letter at a time, demonstrate the sign language gesture for each letter as you introduce it. When you need your students' attention just say, "One, two, three—show me your [B]!" At that point have each child face you and show the sign for that particular letter. Besides reinforcing that letter and the sign, you'll also have each child's attention!

Suzanne Walker Lank
William Perry Elementary, Waynesboro, VA

Quiet Transition

Stuffed animals can help make classroom transition times quiet times. Keep a collection of stuffed animals handy. When you call students to the rug for storytime, ask your Student of the Week to observe his classmates and identify five or more youngsters who move to the story area quickly and quietly. Then have him present each of these students with a stuffed animal that he may hold while the story is being read.

Kerry Ojeda
Paul Ecke Central School, Encinitas, CA

Categories

Do you find yourself getting caught in transition times with just a spare minute or two on your hands? If so, try this activity to engage your students' minds during those moments. In your mind choose a category, such as opposites, rhymes, or food groups. When you need to fill a few spare minutes, say the name of the category. Then, each time you call out that category (such as "Rhymes With Cat"), have your students respond with appropriate words. You can choose categories that are as simple or as complex as your students' abilities will allow.

Jamie Wiklendt, Avondale Elementary School
Avondale Estates, GA

All Wound Up

Do you ever wind up with a roomful of excitable youngsters after certain activities? If so, try using a music box to help your little ones unwind in preparation for the next activity. Wind the music box. While the music is playing, have the children relax by lying down or resting their heads on the tables. When the music stops, students will be calmer and prepared for the next transition.

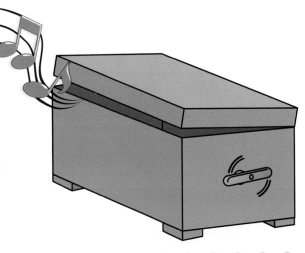

Pablo Millares
Van E. Blanton Elementary, Miami, FL

Transition Time Tally

This transition plan promotes teamwork *and* provides practice counting tally marks. Have each group (or row) of students choose a team name. List the names in the corner of the chalkboard. Each time a team makes a smooth transition between activities, draw a tally mark by its name. When a team earns 15 (or more) tally marks, recognize the team's efforts with a round of applause and, if desired, give each team member a sticker or other small reward. Then erase that team's tallies and challenge the team to earn another set!

Candi Deal, Dalton, GA

Crickets	卌
Ladybugs	卌 l
Bumblebees	llll
Grasshoppers	卌l
Dragonflies	卌 l

Group Captains

If your students are seated in a small-group desk arrangement, use this tip to save time *and* promote smooth transitions! In each group designate one child as the captain for the week. When it's time to collect papers or manipulatives, group members pass their materials to the captain, who then takes responsibility for the items. The group captain also distributes papers and manipulatives to the group. Establish a rotation system that allows each child a turn as captain. Along with having a more efficient classroom, you'll be nurturing responsibility!

Jeannie Hinyard
Welder Elementary, Sinton, TX

All Set? You Bet!

Here's a quick way to find out which students are ready for the next task at hand. Simply ask, "All set?" and snap your fingers twice. The students who are ready respond, "You bet!" The others say, "Not yet." If necessary, wait a few moments; then repeat the question. This upbeat exchange prompts students to ready themselves in a timely manner, without making them feel anxious.

Maryann Chern Bannwart
Antietam Elementary, Woodbridge, VA

Organizational Tips

Contents

Bulletin Boards and Displays

Showcasing Student Work ✓

Finding extra classroom space to display student work just got easier! Hot-glue individual clothespins to poster board stars. Use Velcro strips, Sticky-Tac, magnetic tape, or masking tape to mount the stars on closet doors, file cabinets, windows, walls—any location that's within a youngster's reach and is suitable for displaying papers and projects. Have each child clip a sample of his finest work to a different star. Invite students to update their all-star displays as often as they wish. Everyone's a star!

Cindy Fingerlin
Eisenhower School, Parlin, NJ

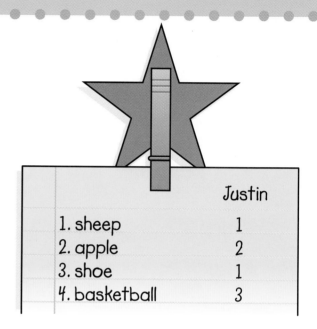

	Justin
1. sheep	1
2. apple	2
3. shoe	1
4. basketball	3

Bulletin Board Borders

Now here's a display idea that's really practical. Purchase off-season borders (which are often discounted); then decorate the back side of the border in the theme of your choice. Simply sponge-paint or stencil the blank side of the border; then allow the border to dry. Mount your border on a bulletin board. Save the border and use the other side when it's in season. Two borders for the price of one!

Linda Shute, Grace Day Care, Lafayette, IN

Extra Display Space

If tape and other adhesives just won't stick to your classroom wall, try this colorful display technique. Sew a ¾-inch casing at one end of a two-yard length of colorful fabric. Insert a ½-inch dowel through the casing. Suspend the resulting banner from the ceiling; then pin on desired items for an eye-catching display.

Betty P. Reynolds
Stewartsville Elementary, Vinton, VA

Display Tip

Do you have trouble displaying children's work on your classroom walls due to high humidity or tape that peels the paint off? Here's a solution: Hot-glue clothespins to your walls where you'd like to display children's work. Then simply clip the work to the clothespins. If you mount some of the clothespins at child height, youngsters can even take responsibility for displaying their own work.

Kathy Lindsey
Waimea Elementary and Intermediate School
Kamuela, HI

Letter Storage

Are you having difficulty keeping up with your bulletin board letters? If so, this tip may be just what you need. Store your bulletin board letters alphabetically in a recipe box or index card file. Locating letters will be as easy as A, B, C.

Erma McGill
Kiowa HeadStart, Kiowa, OK

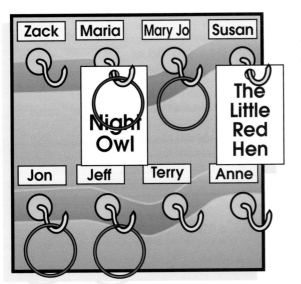

Cup Hook Display

A display with cup hooks can have multiple uses in your classroom! To make this display board, paint or stain a piece of plywood. Every few inches, screw a cup hook into the plywood. Write each child's name on a separate strip of construction paper or labeling tape. Then attach one child's name above each cup hook. Use the cup hook display for taking attendance. For example, as each child enters the room, have him place a ring (the seal from a milk jug) on his hook. Another timesaving way to use this display is to make a card for each book in your class library. Punch a hole near the top of each card. When a student checks out a book, have him hang the corresponding card on his hook. One quick glance at the board will tell you which students have checked out books.

Jan Prince
Booth Elementary School, Enfield, IL

Bulletin Boards and Displays

Shirt Clips

Hanging classroom displays is no longer a chore with this helpful hint. Mount plastic shirt clips (sometimes found on new shirts) on a wall, bulletin board, or any flat surface. Use them to hold memos, students' work, or bulletin board displays. Shirt clips can also be used as a safe alternative to pins when clipping awards, nametags, or badges to students' shirts.

Karen D. Turner
Frankfort, KY

A Bounty of Borders?

Do you need a convenient way to protect and store a bounty of bulletin board borders? Collect a clean, empty plastic frosting container for each border you wish to store. Cut off a sample of the border; then attach it to the front of a container with clear Con-Tact covering. Next, roll up the border and slip it inside the container. Snap on the lid and you're all set!

Mary C. Audsley
Attica Elementary, Attica, NY

Made by Me!

Show off students' art with this picture-perfect display. In advance, take a close-up photograph of each child's face. Cut her head out of the photograph and glue it onto the head of a tagboard child cutout. Personalize the cutout; then hot-glue a wooden, spring clothespin to each hand. Then mount the cutouts on a wall where students can reach them. Invite each child to display her art by clipping it to the clothespins on her cutout.

Laura Leuenberger
Runyan Elementary, Conroe, TX

Sticker Strips

Cash in with this unique sticker display idea! Tape a strip of blank receipt tape at the top of each child's desk. Encourage students to showcase their sticker collections on the tape. Periodically send the collections home and begin new ones. Now that's inexpensive sticker storage that's guaranteed to ring up smiles!

Jennifer Metcalfe, Clara Brenton Public School, London, ON

Calendar Timesaver

Tired of removing staples or masking tape each time you reposition the dates on your monthly calendar? Check your local office supply store for a restickable adhesive glue stick. Apply a generous coating of the adhesive to the back of calendar date cards; then press the dates on the calendar. Since the adhesive is restickable, the dates are easy to reposition. Use the same technique to attach special messages and notes. This is a timesaver you're sure to stick with!

Barbara Turner, Pelham Road Elementary, Greenville, SC

Book Displays

Hung up on how to store and display your collection of classroom books? Try using coat hangers. Mount screws or cup hooks on your wall; then place a hanger on each screw or hook. Open and drape multiple copies of a book over the bar of each hanger. Youngsters can identify, remove, and replace books with ease.

Sheri Dressler
Woodland School
Palatine, IL

Bulletin Boards and Displays

Bag of Borders

Organizing bulletin board borders in a shoe storage bag with clear pockets is a smart idea! Suspend the bag inside a closet door. Roll up your borders and store them in the clear pockets. Now you can find the border you need at a glance!

Debra Culpepper
Cedar Road Elementary
Chesapeake, VA

Bulletin Board Album

Keep a picture-perfect record of bulletin board ideas in a photo album. Each time you decorate a bulletin board, photograph the results. Also photograph other favorite displays that you see around your school and other schools that you visit. Organize the resulting photographs in a photo album. To enhance your collection, cut out bulletin boards featured in teacher magazines. The next time you're searching for that perfect display, you'll have an album full of good ideas to choose from!

Gayla Hammer
West Elementary and South Elementary, Lander, WY

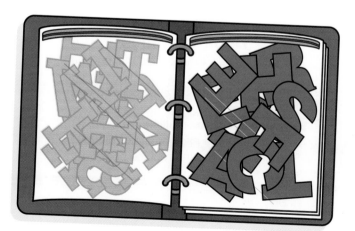

Storing Letter Cutouts

Here's a tip for organizing your bulletin board letters. Sort letters by style, size, and/or color; then place each group of letters in a gallon-size, resealable plastic storage bag. Three-hole-punch the plastic bags as shown and place them in a three-ring notebook. Store the binder in a handy location. The next time you need letter cutouts, you'll have them neatly organized and ready to use!

Angela Virostick
West Hill Elementary
Sharon, PA

Yarn Displays

Do you get all strung out over displays that just won't stick to the walls? If so, put away your tape and try using yarn instead. In compliance with fire safety codes, tie lengths of yarn to hooks mounted near the ceiling. Using clothespins, attach student work along the pieces of yarn. Not only will the work stay in place, but the vertical arrangement makes an interesting display.

Marcia Longo
Hancock North Central Elementary, Pass Christian, MS

Sample Book

To help you remember which shapes can be created on your school's die-cut machine, make a sample book. To do this, gather one sample of each shape. Categorize the shapes as desired; then glue the shapes onto the pages of a blank booklet or spiral notebook. Use divider tabs to label the different sections of the sample book. There you have it—a shipshape sample book!

Karen Bryant, Rosa Taylor Elementary, Macon, GA

Now You See It; Now You Don't!

Did you know that you can erase permanent marker when it's on a laminated surface? Just use a white vinyl eraser and wipe those marks away. Finally, a simple solution to help you reuse calendars, memos, and displays!

Chava Shapiro
Beth Rochel School
Monsey, NY

Filing Systems

Organizing Thematic Materials

To organize collections of thematic materials that span several grade levels, first sort the materials by theme. Next, label a three-ring binder for each theme. Three-hole-punch the lesson plans, reproducibles, magazine articles, and other teaching aids you have collected, and place them in the appropriate binders. When preparing for a thematic unit, you can easily locate materials that will meet the needs of the students you are currently teaching.

Tanya Wilder
Wolf Creek Elementary
Broken Arrow, OK

Unit Record

Organize your teaching units with this handy tip. Complete a one-page unit record listing all of the materials that you have available for a particular unit such as books, films, poems, games, and songs. Once your unit record is complete, use it to speed you along as you write your lesson plans. Reuse this record from year to year. It's a great way to jog your memory about the resources you have collected.

Mary Tamporello
Wyandotte Elementary, Morgan City, LA

Seasonal Activities

Still searching for that terrific art project your students did last Earth Day? Save time and effort looking for each month's special ideas with this organizational tip. On folders labeled for each month of the school year, write the names of your seasonal/monthly activity books and the page numbers of appropriate activities. You'll have all the monthly resources that you need at your fingertips—without the usual mad rush!

Mandy Marr
Florien Elementary School
Florien, LA

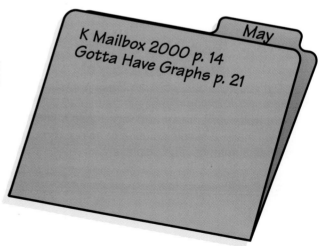

K Mailbox 2000 p. 14
Gotta Have Graphs p. 21

May

Award Binder

Organize your supply of student awards and certificates in a three-ring binder. Place copies of like awards into 9" x 12" plastic protectors. Tape the lower edge of each protector closed; then sort the awards into categories such as good behavior, neatness, and academic achievement. Label a tabbed divider page for each category. Organize the divider pages and protected awards in a binder. When you need an award, open the binder to the appropriate category and make your selection.

Laura Mihalenko
Truman Elementary School, Parlin, NJ

Clutter-Busting Binder

Does it seem as though endless piles of memos and notices end up on your desk? You need a clutter-buster binder! In a three-ring binder place dividers that you have labeled with appropriate topics like "class rosters," "custodial forms," "parent correspondence," and "office memos." Alphabetize the topics for easy reference. When you receive a notice or memo, immediately file it in your binder. Not only will you be more organized, but you'll also be able to see the top of your desk again!

Nancy Lyde, Kiker Elementary School, Austin, TX

Photo Album Organization

No more endless searching for that cute idea that you remember seeing somewhere! Using colored index tabs, label sections of a photo album with categories such as Halloween, Christmas, spring, and animals. Print songs, fingerplays, games, or other ideas on index cards. Slide each card into a slot in the album. Then those ideas are readily available when you need them.

Beth Prawdzik
Somerset School, Troy, MI

Filing Systems

Organizing Student Pictures

If you're struggling with how to keep track of all those handy individual student pictures, use notebook-size slide holders. Photocopy a supply of each child's picture. Then slide each child's photo into a section on the holder. Insert the photocopies behind the original picture. Then, just when you need them for classroom projects, each child's picture will be easily accessible.

Susan Axelrod
Council Rock School, Rochester, NY

Files at Your Fingertips

How often do you momentarily misplace notes from parents because they accidentally become buried under other school-related paperwork? This easy filing system can put a stop to these frightful moments. Label a hanging file folder for each student; then place the folders in a hanging file box that you have positioned within an arm's reach of your desk. When a student hands you a note from her parent(s), read the note; then immediately place it in the student's file. If you need to retrieve the note, you'll know right where to find it.

Leslee McWhirter, Mendel Elementary, Houston, TX

Three-Ring Binder ✓

If your file folders are filled to the brim and you have difficulty locating ideas, then try this filing system. Keep ideas organized in a three-ring binder containing pocket dividers. Label each pocket with its contents, such as art ideas, fingerplays, games, or math activities. In each pocket, store corresponding ideas, lessons, and activities. Using this binder, you'll be able to locate what you need with ease!

Janet Koenig
Riverview Pre/K, Sioux City, IA

Thematic Filing System

Although this system takes a bit of time to get it started, the payoff is definitely worth it! For each theme that you study, label a file folder. Staple three sheets of paper to the inside of the folder. Label the first sheet "Objectives," and record skills associated with that theme. Then label the second sheet "Activities." To ensure that you have balanced ideas, program this page with each of your curriculum areas. Finally, label the last page "Books/Audio/Visuals." As you gather ideas for each theme, record them on the appropriate pages. For example, you might run across a great outdoor game for Turkeys while leafing through a P. E. resource. Immediately record that idea in your Turkey folder under "Gross-Motor Activities." Then, when November rolls around, the idea can be easily located!

Linda Crosby
Hill Crest Community School, Fort Vermilion, Alberta, Canada

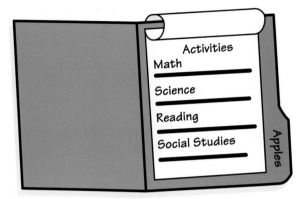

Mailbox Keepsake

Try this organized filing system to centralize your favorite ideas from *The Mailbox* magazine. Attach labeled tabs representing upcoming units to pages from a loose-leaf photo album. Put several pages behind each tab in the album. Clip or photocopy ideas that you want to keep on file. Place the ideas in the appropriate section of the album. This handy reference will make finding ideas a snap.

Amy Pylant
Killarney Elementary, Orlando, FL

Magazine Binders

If your summer to-do list includes organizing your back issues of *The Mailbox®* magazine, try this great tip. Label each of six three-ring binders for a different magazine edition. Three-hole-punch each magazine and place it in the appropriate binder in sequential order. Continue this practice each time you receive a new magazine issue. To make your binders even more usable, keep a photocopy of each end-of-the-year index at the front of your August/September binder.

Joan Hodges, Lantern Lane Elementary, Missouri City, TX

Happy Birthday to You ✓

With all that you have to do in a day, remembering your students' birthdays can be a challenge. If you utilize a little spare time this summer, you will be ahead of the game. As you relax, fill out a class set of birthday cards with best wishes and your signature. In the fall, when you learn the names of your students, address the envelopes. Organize the cards by month. Now that you are so well prepared, you will really feel like celebrating.

Mary Dinneen, Mountain View School, Bristol, CT

Awards/Rewards File

Keep your awards and certificates right at your fingertips with this handy organizational idea. Make a file folder for each award or certificate that you plan to use. Identify each award file by coloring one copy of each award and gluing it to the front of the folder. Laminate the folder and place the original award inside along with several copies. The awards are sorted and ready for giving.

Debra S. Bott
Duson Elementary, Duson, LA

Ideas in the Bag

Here's an easy way to store those great ideas you've jotted down on paper scraps. Staple or tape the sides of a quart-size zippered plastic bag to the inside of a file folder. Then slip the paper pieces inside the bag and zip it shut. When you get ready to plan, just unzip those ideas!

Ashlei B. Lockhart
Dunleith Elementary School
Marietta, GA

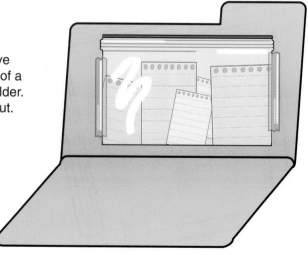

Weekday Files ✓

End those paper pileups with this quick and easy filing system. Label each of five different-colored file folders with a day of the week. Store all papers, books, and other materials needed for a particular day in the appropriate folder. Then all you (or your subsitute) need is your daily folder and you're ready to go!

Terry Schreiber
Holy Family School, Norwood, NJ

Have File, Will Travel

Portable file folders give you a little bit of freedom and also help children develop responsibility—which, in turn, saves you precious time! Instead of using filing cabinets for your students' file folders, use a portable, plastic file box. You can keep these file boxes anywhere in your classroom, allowing children to put their own papers in their files. And if you'd like to transport the files to another more convenient location, they're ready to go!

Karen Griffin, Rainwater Elementary, Carrollton, TX

Movie Picks

Use this organizational tip to save time when you're looking for an appropriate movie or video. Each time you view or hear of a movie that corresponds with one of your themes, write the title on an index card along with any comments and ordering information. Also write the corresponding theme in large letters at the top of the card. File these cards alphabetically in a file box. When you need a movie, simply look through your titles and pick a winner!

Robin Goddard
Mt. Vernon Elementary, St. Petersburg, FL

Transportation

Let's Go!
21 minutes ☆☆Good
Transportation-
mostly land vehicles!

Filing Systems

New Student Welcome File

Make new student arrival easy on yourself and the new child with this handy file! First, label an accordion file "Welcome, New Students!" Then label each of the inner compartments with a different supply that is needed throughout the school year (such as nametags, cubby labels, permission slips, monthly calendars, book-order procedures, etc.). File each supply in its corresponding compartment. When a new student arrives, simply pull one item from each compartment. In no time at all, you and your new student will be up and running!

Karen Griffin
Rainwater Elementary, Carrollton, TX

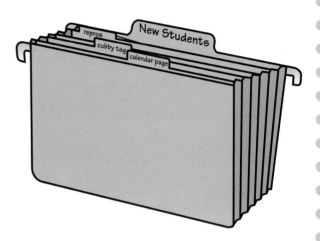

The Borrow Box

Here's an easy way to keep track of classroom materials that you've lent to other teachers. Each time an item is borrowed, write its name and the borrower's name on a small index card. Store the card in a file box. When an item is returned, cross the borrower's name off the card.

Gayla Hammer
West Elementary & South Elementary, Lander, WY

Handy Information Cards ✓

Here's an idea that will keep student information at your fingertips. On a 3" x 5" index card for each youngster, list important information such as the student's name, address, phone number, birthday, parents' names, and emergency information. Punch a hole in the bottom right-hand corner of each card; then put all of the cards on a large metal ring. Fasten the ring onto a drawer handle for easy access. These cards also come in handy when checking students' personal information skills.

Debbie Peters
Avondale Elementary School
Marion, AR

S.O.S. (Save Our Stickers) ✓

Do you find yourself searching through drawers for just the right stickers at just the right time? You'll be stuck on this sticker storage idea! Label the slots in a small accordion file with themes, seasons, etc. Then neatly file your stickers in the appropriate compartments. When you need a certain type of sticker, you'll know just where to look!

Rhonda Foster

Sticker Rings ✓

Save time and minimize clutter by organizing your sticker collection on metal rings. Hole-punch the top of each sticker sheet as you sort the sheets by theme, holiday, or other desired criteria. Then bind each group of stickers onto a separate ring. Your days of sifting through miscellaneous stickers are over!

Heather Volkman
Messiah Lutheran School
St. Louis, MO

Organizing Stickers

Here's an idea that you can bank on. Keep your incentive stickers categorized with a check organizer that is divided into months. In each monthly divider, place stickers appropriate for that month. No more sorting through Christmas trees and jack-o'-lanterns to find your end-of-the-year stickers.

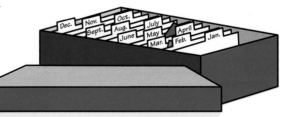

Ann Senn
Welch Elementary
West Monroe, LA

Carpet Capers

In just a few seconds, your youngsters can be sitting pretty right where you want them. For each child, personalize a carpet square by writing his name on a sticky nametag and attaching it to the back of the carpet square. Arrange carpet squares, with the name sides up, in the style best suited to your upcoming activity. Then a youngster simply finds his name, flips the carpet over, and is seated on his carpet square. Any seating arrangement you desire can be achieved in a snap!

Denise Covert
Shepherd of the Valley, Moreno Valley, CA

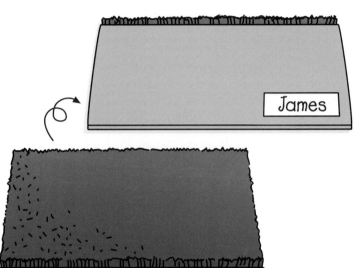

James

Carpet Seating Assignments

Use carpet samples (purchased or donated from a carpet store) to create a large area rug for floor activities. To assemble an area rug, place identically sized carpet pieces facedown so that there are five rows of five pieces. Connect the pieces by taping the seams together using duct tape. Turn the area rug over. Then design a seating arrangement for typical floor activities by assigning each child her own carpet piece. For other types of activities, the patchwork layout of the rug can be used to space youngsters as necessary. For example, have students sit within the first two rows of carpet pieces during storytime or within the last two rows for viewing a video on an elevated TV screen. Your students will be snug as bugs on your new area rug!

Mary Johnson, Grandville Christian School, Grandville, MI

Desk Groupings

Colorful adhesive dots can help keep student desks organized. Choose one desk in each group and affix two adhesive dots to the floor beneath its front legs. Ask the appropriate students to keep these desks properly positioned atop the dots. Instruct the remaining children in each group to align their desks accordingly. Replace and reposition the dots as desired.

Tamra Oliver
Margaret Beeks Elementary
Blacksburg, VA

By the Number

Score big with this classroom management tip. In the corner of each child's desktop (or table space) tape a card labeled with a numeral from 1 to 4. If student desks are arranged in groups, vary the numbers in the group. Use the numbers for a variety of tasks. For example, ask "fours" to collect math manipulatives or "threes" to line up first. Ask every "two" to pair with a "one" and so on. The possibilities are innumerable!

Lia Caprio, Ingleside Elementary, Norfolk, VA

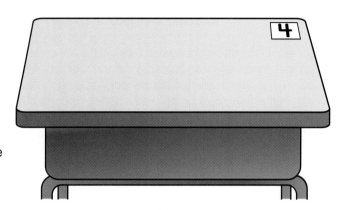

Weekday Grouping

For a practical room arrangement, organize students' desks into five groups or rows; then assign each group a different weekday name. This simple grouping lends itself to many practical uses. Refer to the group names as you call students to line up, hand in papers, or use learning centers. Each day enlist the students in that day's group to help with daily calendar activities and other classroom chores. To limit time spent on show-and-tell, have just the students in the day's group share their treasures. Students will quickly identify with their group names, making it easy for you to implement these routines and many others.

Benita Kuhlman, Avon Public School 4–1, Avon, SD

Reusing Desktags

If changes in your student enrollment make it necessary for you to purchase several sets of desk-tags each year, try this idea. Laminate a class supply (plus a few extras) of unprogrammed desktags. Then, from clear Con-Tact covering, cut a class supply of strips. Each strip should be approximately one inch longer and wider than a desktag. Use the strips to cover and adhere the desktags to your students' desks. Then, writing atop the clear covering, use a permanent marker to personalize each desktag. When a student moves away, peel away the strip of programmed covering. You'll be left with a good-as-new desktag that can be used again and again!

Marie Lain
Marjory Stoneman Douglas Elementary, Miami, FL

Color-Coded Flowerpots

These one-of-a-kind flowerpots are a fun way to color-code groups (or tables) of students' desks. Use a different color of paint to decorate an inexpensive plastic flowerpot for each group. Also make several like-colored tissue-paper flowers per pot. Tape each flower to one end of a wooden skewer or a green pipe cleaner, and attach construction paper leaves to the resulting stems. When the painted pots are dry, put a layer of rocks in the bottom of each one (for added weight). Trim a piece of florist's foam or polystyrene foam to fit inside each pot; then press the foam in place and poke the flower stems into the foam. Present each group of students with a pot-o'-blooms. Just look at that yellow group! Each of its members are ready to begin.

Marie Lain
Marjory Stoneman Douglas Elementary, Miami, FL

Rearrange Your Room for Spring!

This spring, create a fresh look in your classroom by arranging your students' desks into flower shapes. Then name each arrangement for a flower. Encourage each group of students to work together to keep their "flower" beautiful. At the end of the day, award the best flower an artificial bouquet. (This bouquet can be displayed throughout the following day.) Then have students close the petals of their flowers by placing their chairs atop their desks.

Ronna Young, Hawthorne Elementary School, Indianapolis, IN

Table Management Tool

Here's a great management idea to use when your students are working at tables. Number each table and color-code each student's table space. Refer to table numbers when praising groups of students who are exhibiting positive behaviors. When it is time to tidy up, call out a color. All students who are represented by the color chosen are responsible for cleanup duty. Your room will be spiffy in a jiffy!

Mae Purrenhage
Jackson Elementary, Fort Campbell, KY

Teacher's Tool Belt

Try this idea when you need supplies right at your fingertips. Purchase a muslin tool belt from a hardware store. Sponge-paint or stencil the pockets of the tool belt with the designs of your choice. Place frequently used items such as stickers, pens, markers, glue, and scissors in the pockets of the tool belt. Since supplies are right at hand when you are sporting your teacher's tool belt, valuable time is saved.

Nancy Smith
Capac Elementary, Washington, MI

Pack It

Keep your teaching essentials at your fingertips in a spill-proof belt pack. Fill a belt pack with a pair of scissors, a glue stick, stickers, and other items that you frequently use throughout the day. Zip it closed, strap on the belt pack, and you'll be organized and ready to face a busy day.

Karen Richards and Carol Fleck, Red Bug Elementary, Longwood, FL

Get Organized! Bag It!

Organize desk items using the wide variety of gift bags that are available. Each month place a different bag on your desk to store notepads, stickers, nametags, and awards. Use seasonal and holiday bags such as a bunny bag for Easter or a flower bag for spring. This is a fun and festive way to dress up your desk and to end clutter.

Susan M. Nutzman
North Elementary School
Falls City, NE

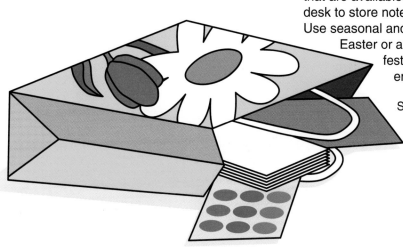

Storage

Box It Up

Use this tip to keep a week's worth of materials organized. Collect sturdy, flat boxes or tubs (such as plastic dishpans) and label each one with a different day of the week. As you plan for each day, place all the needed supplies into the appropriate boxes. With this storage system, you won't lose precious time searching for materials. These handy boxes are particularly useful for substitutes, since everything they need is in one place.

Jan Harding
Crescent Elementary, Sandy, UT

Storage by Theme

Use this suggestion and your teaching materials will always be in place. Organize your lesson plans, bulletin-board materials, art projects, reproducibles, and centers by storing them by theme. Place all of the materials in a storage box and label the outside of the box with the theme and the contents of the box. With this system, all of your materials will be in one spot and monthly planning will be simplified.

Julia Endriss
Hale Aloha Nazarene School, Hilo, HI

Pizza Box Storage

Any way you slice it, a pizza-box storage system really stacks up. Store flat, oversized seasonal and holiday cutouts in large, labeled pizza boxes. These sturdy boxes hold many cutouts and stack neatly in closets or on shelves.

Barb Hunt
Kinderhouse, Cedarville, OH

Bag It!

This timesaving idea will suit any busy teacher. You need a clear, plastic suit bag labeled for each month (or season) of the school year. When you take down your end-of-the-year classroom decorations, store them in the appropriate suit bag along with any other over-sized (or hard-to-store) teaching materials for that time of year. Then sort the classroom decorations and over-sized teaching materials that are stored elsewhere in the classroom into the labeled bags. Suspend the bags in a classroom closet. Just think of the time you'll save next year when you have a clear view of each bag's contents!

Denise Baumann, Rustic Oak Elementary, Pearland, TX

Extra Storage

Empty laundry detergent boxes make great storage containers. Cut off the lids and handles of the detergent boxes, and attach the boxes to create compartments to store your youngsters' papers, workbooks, or magazines. They work perfectly for organizing work by the day of the week or for substitute teachers.

Kathy Curnow
Woolridge Elementary, Midlothian, VA

Monthly Boxes

No more endless searching for ideas when you organize your classroom materials in monthly storage boxes. Collect a box with a lid for each month that you teach. Label the outside of each box with a different month; then store your seasonal books, games, decorations, and centers inside the appropriate box. List the contents of each box on a piece of tagboard; then glue the tagboard onto the side of the box. Now all of your seasonal materials will be right at your fingertips.

Elaine Galeazzi
Trabert Center, Knoxville, IA

Add-On Hangers

Use add-on hangers to organize posters, charts, and small centers. Clip the materials to the hangers using both sides and link the hangers together. Your materials are right at your fingertips and it proves to be a real space saver.

Pat Marr
Taft School
Ferndale, MI

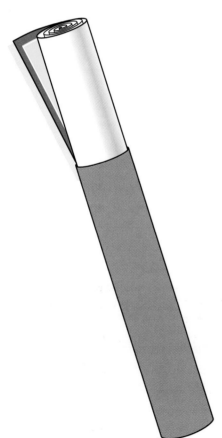

Theme Chart Storage

Save wrapping paper and paper towel tubes for storing charts and posters that go with your themes. Roll up a chart or poster, and place it inside a tube. Label the outside of the tube with the theme title and store the tube in the corresponding theme box. Classroom charts and posters will be easily accessible and well protected.

Faith Shiver
Lillian E. Williams Elementary School
Attapulgus, GA

Topics at Your Fingertips

Have you collected so many resource books over the years that you don't even know where to begin looking through them? Here's a tip to help organize that colossal collection. Arrange your books according to topics—reading, math, centers, art, etc. Using a different color of sticker dots for each topic, attach a dot to the spine of each book. (For example, all reading books might have blue dots on them.) To be sure that the dots stay on the books, cover them with transparent tape. Then arrange the books according to topic (color dot) on a bookshelf or in a file. If desired, make a legend showing each color and topic for your reference. Then, when you need ideas for specific topics, you'll know exactly where to look!

Jeanne A. Nye
C. O. Greenfield, Phoenix, AZ

A Dot Marks the Spot

It's often difficult to keep track of resources gathered from a variety of locations. Simplify this process by color-coding your resources with easy-to-remove adhesive dots. Attach colored dots to borrowed materials in a manner such as:

red dots   = school library
yellow dots = public library
blue dots   = colleagues

A quick glance at each borrowed item quickly identifies its place of origin. Remove the dots before returning the materials and reuse them as desired.

Cheryl P. Chartrand, Glenfield Elementary, Lowville, NY

Library Organization

To organize your classroom library in a snap, use the following color/alphabet code to label adhesive dots: blue dot labeled *B* to indicate biography, red dot labeled *F* to indicate fiction, yellow dot labeled *N* to indicate nonfiction, green dot labeled *E* to indicate everybody (easy-to-read). Then, using a length of clear packaging tape, adhere an appropriate dot to the spine of each book. Categorize the books on the bookshelves and your task is complete!

Kara Coffman, Forcey Christian School, Silver Spring, MD

Rackin' Up Big Books

Looking for inexpensive, child-accessible storage for your big books? If you have a little-used laundry drying rack at home or see one at a yard sale, there's your answer! If desired, spray-paint the rack; then screw the legs onto a sheet of plywood. Hang your big books—front cover facing out—on the upper rungs of the rack. Hang earphones, bags of little books, and audio cassettes on the lower rungs. Big-book storage doesn't get any easier than this!

Catherine Turpin
Mohave Valley Elementary School
Bullhead City, AZ

Coffee Tin Organizers

All of those hard-to-keep-track-of school supplies can be right where you want them with this creative reuse of small flavored coffee tins and lids. Place empty coffee tins in your desk drawer. In each tin, store a different item such as paper clips, thumbtacks, rubber bands, chalk, safety pins, and brads. Seal each tin with a lid labeled with that tin's contents. Celebrate the moments that you'll save looking for supplies!

Debra S. Bott, Duson Elementary, Scott, LA

Keep It Neat

Try this tip for keeping cabinets, shelves, and learning-center areas tidy. Organize and then photograph the areas of your classroom that often become cluttered. Mount the snapshots in the corresponding areas. When children return games, puzzles, books, and other supplies to these areas, they can refer to the snapshots for proper placement of the returned items. It works like a charm! The photographs will also come in handy when you are setting up your classroom next fall.

Alyce Pearl Smith
Butzbach Elementary, Germany

Crayon Cans

Corral loose crayons with crayon cans. To make two crayon cans, cut a clean, lidded Pringles potato chip can into three equal sections. Discard the middle section. Cover the two resulting cans with decorated, laminated strips. Fill each can with crayons. Now little fingers can easily select the crayons that they need and replace them when they're finished.

Roxanne Rast, Big Sky School, Billings, MT

Crayon Holders

When your youngsters' crayon boxes have become too flimsy or you need a home for runaway crayons, powdered drink mix containers are just the ticket. Store crayons in lidded drink mix containers. Little hands can open the containers and reseal them for the safekeeping of the items inside.

Debbie Earley
Mountain View Elementary School, Kingsley, PA

Colorful Crayon Holders

Reinforce visual discrimination and also organize crayons with these neat crayon holders. Collect eight half-pint milk cartons for each table or station. Use construction paper to cover each milk carton in one set with one of the eight basic colors. Staple these eight cartons together to make one crayon holder. Repeat the process to assemble the remaining holders. Using self-adhesive labels, label the outside of each carton with its color's name. Sort a supply of crayons into each holder. Place a crayon holder on each table.

Alana Holley
Windmill Point Elementary
Port St. Lucie, FL

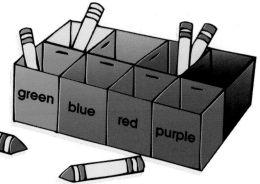

Where's My Pencil?

Do your youngsters often lose or misplace their pencils? Eliminate this problem with self-adhesive Velcro tape. Cut a length of Velcro tape long enough to wrap around a pencil. Peel the paper off the back of the Velcro pieces. Wrap the loop side around the top of each child's pencil and mount the hook side inside his desk or on his tabletop. When a child is not using his pencil, he simply attaches the pencil to his desk or tabletop. This simple technique is sure to keep pencils right at your youngsters' fingertips.

Shari O'Shea
Conewago Elementary School
Elizabethtown, PA

Velcro

Missing Pencils?

Attaching two pieces of personalized strapping tape to each of your pencils in the fashion shown (see illustration) has several advantages. Students and co-workers instantly know that the pencils belong to you, the pencils will not roll, and the pencils can easily be clipped to a clipboard. Your supply of pencils is certain to last longer!

Marge Westrich
Colby Elementary School, Colby, WI

Piece Pack

Where are those dice when you need them? Scattered board-game pieces, chips, dice, and the like are always in the right spot if you use piece packs. To make one piece pack, adhere one side of a strip of Velcro to a resealable plastic bag. Adhere the other side to the game box or the back of the gameboard. When a child finishes with a game, have him put all of the loose pieces in the bag. Then have him attach the bag to the back where the corresponding strip of Velcro is located. The next time your students want to play a game that requires pieces, they'll know right where to find them!

Melissa Franko, Crown Point, IN

Bits and Pieces

If you find your classroom floor constantly peppered with stray pieces from puzzles, toys, and games, here's a simple way to keep track of those lost bits and pieces. Set aside a special tub for miscellaneous parts. When someone runs across a stray piece, simply toss it into the tub. Then, at a convenient time, choose a helper to find the corresponding places for the pieces in the tub. Finally, a way to make peace with the pieces!

Donna Leonard, Monticello, IA

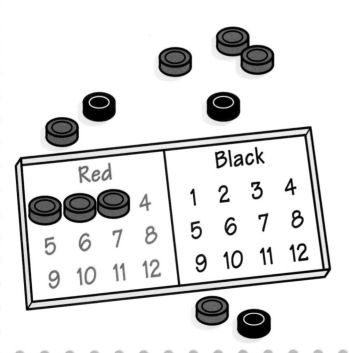

Places for Pieces

Do stray game pieces seem to find their way into the nooks and crannies of your classroom rather than their respective game boxes? Here's a tip to help. On the lid of a game box (or on a cut-to-size sheet of tagboard), make a matching board for each specific game. For checkers, for example, write "Red" on one half of the board, and the numerals 1–12. Repeat the process using "Black" on the other half. When children are ready to clean up, they simply match the playing pieces to the board. When each space is covered, they know they've got all the pieces and the game is ready to be stored.

Mary E. Maurer
Children's Corner Preschool
Durant, OK

Puppets in Pockets

If you're looking for a practical, yet attractive way to store puppets, this tip is for you! Obtain a clear, plastic shoe-storage bag with pockets sized to hold children's shoes. Display the bag so that your youngsters have access to the bag; then poke a puppet in each empty pocket. Your youngsters are sure to enjoy the easy access to the puppets. And a quick glance will tell you which puppets are in use.

Pauline Lawson
Fuquay-Varina Elementary
Fuquay-Varina, NC

Behind Door Number One...

Help students be more independent by labeling your cabinet doors with numerals. Refer to the door numbers when you instruct students to retrieve or put away supplies. For example: "Get the paint from behind door number five." It's a quick trick for strengthening numeral recognition too!

Debbie Bryant
Ball Ground Elementary School, Ball Ground, GA

Puppet Holder

Conveniently display classroom puppets on a plastic, freestanding shoe rack. Slip each puppet over a plastic loop on the shoe rack. Your youngsters will have easy access to puppets when using this helpful hint.

Lois A. Waltz
St. Ambrose School
Old Bridge, NJ

Hook on It!

Coat hooks mounted too high or too sparsely can be chaos in a classroom! Solve the problem with hooks. Screw one cup hook in the underside of a coat closet shelf for each extra hook needed. From each cup hook, hang a personalized closet organizer as shown. Getting everything within your little ones' reach will help promote independence and responsibility as well as a more pleasant classroom environment.

Gayle Young
Evans Elementary School
Evans, GA

Storage List

Keeping track of the supplies you need will be an easy task with this organizational tip. Write a list of your classroom supplies on a sheet of paper and make multiple copies. Keep a copy of the list on the inside of a cupboard door and anywhere else supplies are stored. Whenever you run out of a particular item, mark the item on the list. On your next shopping trip, take the lists with you; then replace each list with a new one.

Mary E. Maurer, Children's Corner, Durant, OK

Gathering Your Thoughts

Does a smattering of thoughts cross your mind during the day, only to be forgotten when you have time to commit them to memory? Here's an idea that will help you gather those stray thoughts and ideas. Always keep a notebook and pencil readily accessible in your classroom. When you're in the middle of painting (for example) and realize that you need to order more green paint, write it down right then in the notebook. You can even ask ambitious youngsters to write certain things in there for you. There you go—all your thoughts in one place!

Lanice McElwain, Falkner Elementary, Falkner, MS

Storage

Clothespin Clippers

Here's a simple solution for labeling students' wet paintings and keeping all of their completed papers together until it's time to go home. Write each student's name on a different clothespin. Throughout the day, encourage each youngster to put each of his completed papers in his clothespin clip. At the end of the school day, have each student transport his papers and projects to his bookbag with the clothespin still attached. This method helps each student keep his papers together and eliminates the need for writing his name on wet artwork.

Kathleen A. Mullane, Middleport Elementary, Middleport, NY

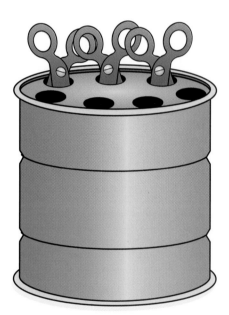

Scissors Storage Can

If you want a practical and safe way to store scissors, this idea may be just what you need. For each table of students, turn a large empty can upside down. In the bottom of the can, drill a quantity of holes that are big enough for the pointed ends of students' scissors to fit through. Insert scissors in the holes, and put a can on each table. Since the scissors are in central locations, youngsters can get right to work.

Cindy Linton
Tuppers Plains Elementary School, Vincent, OH

Desk Pockets

Help students stay organized with colorful desk pockets. To create a class set of pockets, personalize a file folder for each student. Keeping the folders folded, laminate each one. Trim away the laminating film, leaving a ¼-inch margin. To convert each folder into a pocket, use an X-acto knife to slit the laminating film. Then attach each student's folder to his desk with a strip of clear Con-Tact paper or packing tape. Ask students to keep unfinished work in their pockets. At the end of the day, any papers remaining in the pockets are taken home as homework. The colorful folders are also a nifty place for students to display their sticker collections.

Robin Polson-Avra, New Caney Elementary, New Caney, TX

Storing Supplies

Put an end to students fishing through their desks looking for hidden supplies. Personalize a resealable plastic bag for each student; then punch a hole in each bag directly below its seal. Have each youngster seal the supplies he does not use on a daily basis inside his bag. Use metal rings to suspend the bags from plastic clothes hangers—one hanger per row or group of student desks. Store the hangers in an easily accessible location. When the supplies are needed, select students to retrieve and distribute the supply bags for their groups.

Margaret Ann Rhem
Western Branch Intermediate, Chesapeake, VA

Bookbags On Hand

Try this idea for those chaotic moments when a child realizes she has forgotten her bookbag or another child simply doesn't have one. Save the sturdy, plastic drawstring bags that you get from department stores or shoe stores. Keep them on hand in your classroom. When you need a bookbag in a hurry, grab one of these bags and your problem is solved.

Alice Wood, Stroud Elementary School, Stroud, OK

Mailboxes

Help your youngsters keep their papers organized with individual student mailboxes. Obtain several empty divided bottle boxes from a grocery or liquor store. Tape several of the boxes together to make a large mailbox unit. Cover the outsides of the boxes with decorative Con-Tact paper. Using self-adhesive labels, label each compartment of the box with a child's name. Have paper monitors place papers, art projects, and notes in the correct mailboxes. Your students will love the idea of receiving mail!

Kathy Nulty
Greenwood Lake Elementary School, Greenwood Lake, NY

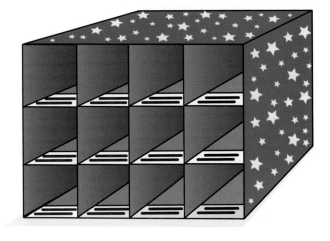

Shoe Organizer Storage

Shoe organizers with see-through pockets provide excellent classroom storage. I hang an organizer inside my closet door and store pipe cleaners, pom-poms, cotton balls, and other art supplies in the pockets. An organizer attached to a magnetic bulletin board is also perfect for holding chalk, manipulatives, hall passes, and other miscellaneous items. Materials are always in view and right at your fingertips!

Geniene Moore
North Columbia Elementary
Appling, GA

Play Dough Recipe

Tired of looking for a play dough recipe each time you want to use one? If so, try this timesaving tip. Using a permanent marker, program a play dough container with your favorite play dough recipe. This will save you lots of time and will be easy for parents, substitutes, and fellow teachers to locate.

Angela Anderson
Richland County Cooperative Preschool, Mansfield, OH

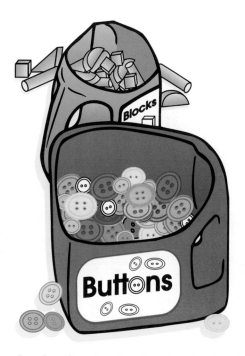

Carryall Jugs

Use this idea for easy-to-carry manipulative storage. Collect a supply of large, empty, and clean laundry-detergent jugs. Saw the top off each jug and file the rough edges with an emery board or cover them with masking tape. Cover the old label with white Con-Tact paper. Then use colorful permanent markers to label each jug and illustrate its new contents. These jugs are perfect for kindergartners because they are easy to carry, materials are visible, and cleanup is a snap!

Elesa Miller
St. Catherine Laboure School
Wheaton, MD

No More Tangles!

Here's a neat way to store skeins of yarn and eliminate those tangled messes. Cut a cross (+) in the center of a Pringles potato crisps lid. Put the yarn in the can; then pull one section of it through the slits in the lid. Replace the lid. Then children will be able to pull out just the amount of yarn that they need without getting it all tangled up.

Valerie Cumpian
Windermere Elementary
Pflugerville, TX

Catch of the Day!

Fishing for a way to organize counters, markers, pens, and other supplies you use with the overhead projector? Try a tackle box! Purchase a tackle box with movable sections that can be customized to hold your items. Keep the box on the overhead projector cart and you'll never have to cast around for supplies again!

Todd Helms, Pinehurst Elementary, Pinehurst, NC

Picture Storage

Try this picture-perfect way to store your youngsters' photocopied photographs. In advance, purchase a hardware storage unit containing lots of miniature drawers. Photocopy a supply of each youngster's school photograph. Place each child's set of photos in a personalized drawer with his photo mounted on the outside of the drawer. When a student needs to use a photograph to personalize artwork or for graphing, he simply locates his drawer and takes out a picture.

Diane Harte
Swegles Elementary, St. John's, MI

Emily Smith

Storage

Hold It!

Keep all those little classroom items from ending up on the floor—use coffee filters! They're great for holding snacks, math manipulatives, and small art supplies. Invite students who finish early to color, cut, or paint their filters. You'll find endless uses for these convenient and inexpensive holders!

Kathy Shaw
Roanoke, VA

Janet Moody
J. W. Faulk Elementary School
Lafayette, LA

Sentence-Strip Storage

Sentence strips are so useful and so handy—but so awkward to store! Well, straighten things out with a long-stemmed flower box. Many florists will donate one for classroom use. It's a perfect fit and can hold quite a lot!

Diane Parette, Durham Elementary, Durham, NY

Circle Tracers Galore

Why can't you ever find the exact size circle tracer when you need it? Now you can! Collect various sizes of plastic lids. Punch a hole in each lid. Then store all the lids on a large metal ring. There you go!

Connie Allen
Immanuel Lutheran School
Manitowoc, WI

Contents

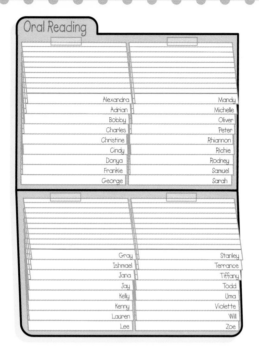

Oral Reading

Alexandra	Mandy
Adrian	Michelle
Bobby	Oliver
Charles	Peter
Christine	Rhiannon
Cindy	Richie
Donya	Rodney
Frankie	Samuel
George	Sarah

Gray	Stanley
Ishmael	Terrance
Jana	Tiffany
Jay	Todd
Kelly	Uma
Kenny	Violette
Lauren	Will
Lee	Zoe

Handy Record Keeping

Gathering details about individual student performance becomes easier when you use these nifty record-keeping folders. To make a folder, label a closed file folder with the skill or behavior you wish to monitor. Inside the folder tape a class set of 3" x 5" lined index cards as shown. Label one index card per student. When you wish to record an observation, open the folder and flip to the appropriate child's card. In no time at all you'll have a wealth of information for parent conferences and report cards.

Pat Hart
C. A. Henning School, Troy, IL

Record Keeping

As you correct papers, keep track of your students' strengths and weaknesses in a spiral notebook. Label an index tab for each child and affix it to the edge of a page. Allow two or three pages for comments about each child. When you discover that a child is excelling or having difficulty with a particular skill, make note of it in the notebook. Your notes will be a great help as you prepare for conferences and report cards.

Carol A. Loveland
Randall Consolidated School, Bassett, WI

Bunny's Book of Big Achievements

To keep track of individual student progress, create a bunny shape booklet for each child. Program each booklet page to represent a pair of basic skills, and leave several spaces after each skill for periodic notations. Children will be proud to take their completed bunny books home to show their parents how much they have learned.

Sandy Burchette
Newport Grammar School
Newport, TN

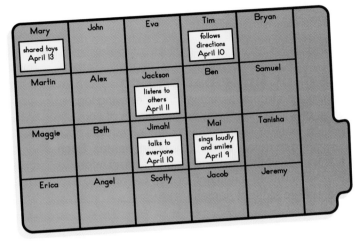

Anecdotal Recording ✓

Keep track of anecdotal comments with this quick recording system. Draw lines inside a file folder to visually divide it into approximately three-inch squares. Label each box with a child's name. During the day, record anecdotal notes on small self-sticking notes, and attach each note to the appropriate child's box. At the end of the day or week, you can quickly transfer the notes to each child's individual records. This system will provide you with a variety of specific notes for your own reference and parent conferences.

Linda Crosby
Hill Crest Community School
Fort Vermilion, Alberta, Canada

Pupils' Progress

This color-coded grading system enables you to instantly interpret your students' progress. After recording your youngsters' scores or grades in your grade book, use colored pencils to lightly color over each entry. Use the following code: A=green, B=yellow, C=blue, D or F=red. Then a quick glance at your grade book can give you the information you need.

Sherrel Rudy, Hoover Elementary, Tulsa, OK

Record-Keeping Displays

Decorating your room with your students' achievements serves two purposes: you'll have attractive room displays and record keeping at a glance! For each skill that you'd like to include, write each child's name on a separate corresponding cutout. For example, use a piggy-bank cutout for recognizing coins, a clock cutout for telling time, and a book cutout for saying the alphabet. For each different skill, mount a colorful title and related artwork on a bulletin board or wall. As each child masters a particular skill, mount her cutout in the appropriate area. To assess each student's progress, you need only look around the room!

Sara Yetter, Saint Jo Elementary, Saint Jo, TX

Oct. 18

Stephen
Bobby
Mariah
Heather
Tambra
Connie
Tricia
Matt
Jennifer

Student Information Log

Keep track of daily information using this timesaving log. On the last page of a legal-size pad, list the names of your students in the left margin. Then cut away the left margin of each remaining page to reveal the list of student names. Each day, date a blank page of the pad and record desired information (such as attendance, behavior, or skill performance) beside the appropriate student names.

Angel Bentley
Auburn Elementary
Auburn, GA

Organizing Student Work

Here's an effective way to minimize paperwork and stay organized! Label a file folder for each student; then number each youngster's folder to match his listing in your grade book. During the day have students place their completed work inside their folders. At the end of the day, collect the folders in numerical order. Grade the folders in this order so that student scores can easily be recorded in your grade book. In addition, any graded papers you wish to place in student files will also be in alphabetical order. If desired, leave graded work that is to be taken home inside the folders. As soon as the folders are distributed the following morning, students can review their work from the previous day, then place it in their cubbies for safekeeping.

Allison Dubson
North Miami Elementary
Miami Beach, FL

Duke Okeke

Grade-Book Tip

This color-coded system allows you to quickly identify which grades in your grade book indicate test scores, homework assignments, or daily work. Before recording a set of grades, use a highlighter and the following code to color the grade-book column you are about to use: yellow=homework assignments, green=daily work, orange=test scores. This system streamlines grade averaging and is helpful when evaluating students' study habits.

Barbara Gusler
Bent Mountain Elementary School
Bent Mountain, VA

Record Keeping Made Easy

Simplify daily record keeping with adhesive labels. Write each child's name on a different label. Throughout the day, jot down anecdotal notes about each child on his label. Then transfer the label to that child's page in a loose-leaf binder. Record keeping has never been easier!

Hope Zabolinsky
Paul Robeson Community School, New Brunswick, NJ

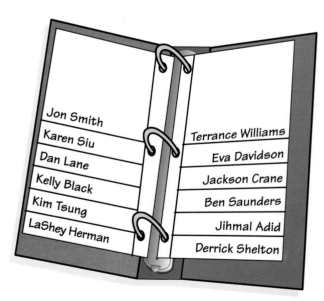

Jon Smith
Karen Siu
Dan Lane
Kelly Black
Kim Tsung
LaShey Herman

Terrance Williams
Eva Davidson
Jackson Crane
Ben Saunders
Jihmal Adid
Derrick Shelton

Tracking Student Progress

Keep an up-to-date record of your students' individual progress right at your fingertips! Purchase a flip-top photo album like the one shown. Personalize a card for each student and insert each card in a plastic sleeve. When you wish to make a note about or check on a student's progress, his card is readily available.

Paige Brannon
Pitt County Schools, Greenville, NC

Centers

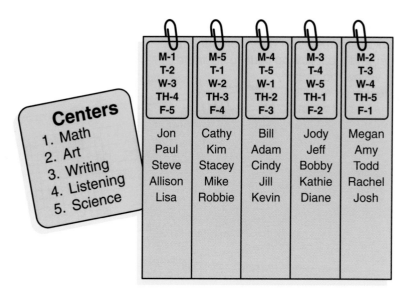

Centers
1. Math
2. Art
3. Writing
4. Listening
5. Science

M-1 T-2 W-3 TH-4 F-5	M-5 T-1 W-2 TH-3 F-4	M-4 T-5 W-1 TH-2 F-3	M-3 T-4 W-5 TH-1 F-2	M-2 T-3 W-4 TH-5 F-1
Jon Paul Steve Allison Lisa	Cathy Kim Stacey Mike Robbie	Bill Adam Cindy Jill Kevin	Jody Jeff Bobby Kathie Diane	Megan Amy Todd Rachel Josh

Center Rotation

This handy chart allows you to easily rotate groups of students to different learning centers. Divide your students into five groups. Visually divide a piece of poster board into five columns. In each column, list the members of one group. (See the illustration.) Next, label each center with a letter or number. Using this code, program a weekly center schedule for each of the five groups. Clip the schedules to the poster board chart. Display the chart and the center code side by side. To change center assignments, either rotate the existing cards or attach new cards to the chart.

Dianne Knight
Frank C. Whiteley School
Hoffman Estates, IL

Colored Clothespins

Since clothespins are often used for a variety of matching games and centers, this tip might be just what you need to keep them organized. Dye a quantity of wooden clothespins by mixing one package of fabric dye and hot water in an old pan. Place the clothespins in the dye for a few minutes; then rinse them with cold water. Using different colors of dye, tint additional clothespins. Use each color of clothespins with a different center. If a clothespin gets separated from its center, you can see at a glance where it belongs!

Carol J. McClintick
Sanford Elementary School, Midland, MI

Organizing Centers

Organize materials for your daily center activities in a jiffy! Establish a color for each of your learning centers; then color-code a resealable plastic storage bag to match each center. In each center bag, place the materials that are needed to complete the center. When center time is over, ask one child at each center to seal the remaining center materials in the center bag.

Cindy Wood
Cedar Lake Christian Academy
Biloxi, MS

Colorful Centers

With this color-coded system of learning center assignments, your little ones will know at a glance where to go for center time. From construction paper cut a large crayon of a different color for each center in your classroom. For each child cut a set of smaller crayons to correspond to the colors of each center. (The small crayons may be cut from construction paper or bulletin board border.) Punch a hole in the top left-hand corner of each crayon cutout. Use a key tag to hold each set of cutouts together. Label each tag with a child's initials. Then label a pegboard with each student's name. With the color of his assigned center in front, hang the child's set of crayons on his peg. When center time arrives, each child can check his peg for the color of his assigned center. Before the next center time, flip a new color to the front of each child's set to give him the opportunity to visit a different center. What a colorful idea!

Trudy White
Mayflower Elementary, Mayflower, AR

Picture Perfect

Labeling classroom learning centers is easy with the help of inexpensive, clear acrylic picture frames. Write the title and directions for each learning activity on an index card; then slip each card into a different frame. Place the frames at the corresponding learning centers. When it's time to change an activity, simply slide the card out of the frame and replace it with a new set of directions. Your centers will be neat and organized, and students will easily see the directions for each activity.

Liz Kramer
Boyden School, Walpole, MA

> Pretty Patterns
> 1. Use the blocks to make a pattern
> 2. Draw and color the pattern on your paper.

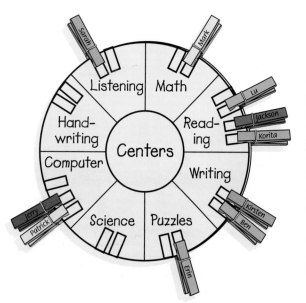

Center Selections

Here's an easy way to avoid overcrowded learning centers. Write the name of each classroom center on a poster board circle like the one shown. Along the edge of each circle section, draw one or more rectangles to show how many students can work at the center at one time. Laminate the resulting center wheel and display it within students' reach. A student clips a personalized clothespin in an empty rectangle on the center wheel and then visits the corresponding center. When she leaves the center, she removes her clothespin. It's a snap!

Mary E. Hoffmann
Camp Avenue Elementary
North Merrick, NY

Center Punch Card

To ensure your youngsters' participation in each classroom center, try this technique. Label each of your centers with a shape cutout—having no two identical shapes the same color. For each child, program and color a construction paper strip with the corresponding shapes. During center time, have each student carry his strip from station to station. When he has completed a center, punch the matching shape on his strip and have him select his next station. Encourage students to visit each of the centers represented on their strips and have their strips punched accordingly. It's easy to see at a glance which centers a student still needs to visit.

Barbara Pasleyn, Energy Elementary, Energy, IL

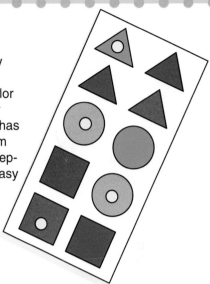

Checking Centers

Enlist the help of your students for checking learning-center work. Check the work of the first child to complete the center. If his work is correct, write the student's name on a list at the center. (If the work is not correct, continue checking student work until a correct version is identified.) When the next child completes the center, she reads the name on the list and asks that child to check her work. If her work is correct, she adds her name to the list. Each child thereafter does the same thing, having the child whose name is last on the list check her work. Children love to help their classmates and you'll love the extra time!

Linda Madron, Mary D. Lang Elementary, Kennett Square, PA

Center Management

Making center assignments is a snap with this proven method. Using clear Con-Tact paper squares, attach a different construction-paper shape to each of several empty, plastic, one-gallon ice cream containers. Place a center activity inside each container. Label your center storage shelves with a second set of matching shapes. Then attach a third set of matching shapes to laminated paper strips. Personalize a clothespin for each youngster. To make center assignments, clip each youngster's clothespin to a shape on the strips. A youngster finds his clothespin on the strip, removes the matching center container from the shelves, completes the activity, and then replaces the container on the shelves where indicated by the matching shape. Youngsters will gain confidence as they complete their center activities independently.

Ann Rowe, Omaha Public Schools, Omaha, NE

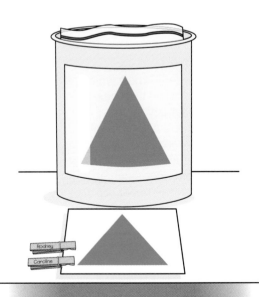

Spin-a-Center

Motivate your children to complete a variety of learning centers with a learning center wheel. To make a wheel, divide a tagboard circle into sections. Write the name of a learning center in each section. Use a brad to attach a pencil-shaped spinner to the center of the cutout. When a child completes his assigned work, he spins the wheel to determine which center to complete.

Leigh Anne Newsom
Greenbrier Intermediate
Chesapeake, VA

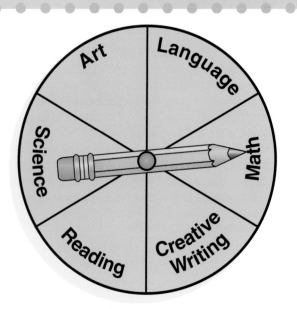

Learning Center Record Keeping

To make sure youngsters have equal opportunities to use your learning centers, try this record-keeping system. Place a class roster at each center. After completing a center, a child crosses off his name. A student may repeat a center after all of his classmates have had a chance to participate.

June Blair, Franklin Elementary School, Reisterstown, MD

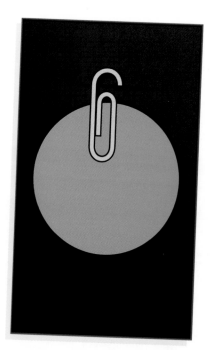

Stop or Go?

Here's a simple tip to let your students know which centers are open for use and which are closed for the time being. For each center, cut out a black or yellow construction paper rectangle (traffic light). Also cut out a green circle and an identically sized red circle for each center. Glue each green circle to a red circle. Then make a small slit in each traffic light as shown. Slide a paper clip through the slit. Post each traffic light near a center. If the center is open for use, slide the circle under the paper clip with the green side showing. If the center is closed, show the red side. So easy to know if it's stop or go!

Kimberly Armbruster
Grace Lane Kindergarten, Coram, NY

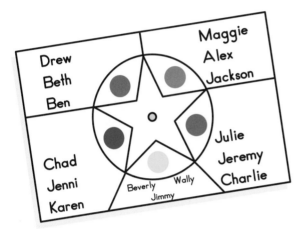

Center Wheel

Are you going around in circles trying to keep up with center assignments? Make a center wheel! First, cut from tagboard a circle and a larger rectangle. Visually divide the circle and the rectangle into the same number of sections as there are groups in your class. Attach a different-colored stick-on dot to each section of the circle. (Each color represents a different center.) Program each section of the rectangle with the names of the children in the different groups. Attach the circle to the rectangle with a brad. Turn the wheel each time you request that the groups change centers. You'll know at a glance where everyone should be.

Janet Fair, Washington School, Beardstown, IL

Center Rotation

Do your students have difficulty remembering which learning center to go to each day? Eliminate the confusion with this simple plan. Divide your students into a desired number of groups (one group per center). Assign each group a shape such as a yellow star or a blue square; then suspend each shape at a center. When a child enters the classroom, he looks for his shape and immediately knows which center to go to. Rotate the center shapes daily in a clockwise direction; then change the center activities at the end of each complete rotation. For easy management, have students keep their assigned shapes throughout the year.

Patricia J. Hamilton, Kempsville Elementary, Virginia Beach, VA

Organizing Individual Centers

Need to organize your individual centers? If so, try this management aid. Store the pieces of individual centers—such as lotto, tangrams, beans, bingo, or buttons—in different gallon-size resealable plastic bags. Label the outside of each bag with its contents. Place four or five bags in a cardboard magazine holder. Then arrange the magazine holders on a table so youngsters have easy access to the centers.

Sue Elliott
Ruskin Elementary School
Ruskin, FL

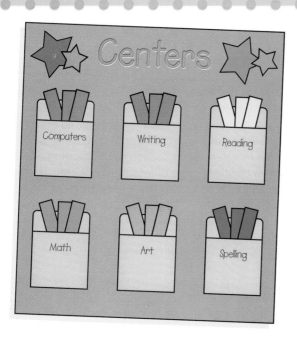

Center Management

If you have centers that are consistently overcrowded, try this center management chart. First, determine how many students can occupy each center at one time. Label one library pocket per center. Then label one paper strip per center occupant. Glue the library pockets to a sheet of poster board and slip the strips in the corresponding pockets. To visit a center, a student takes a paper strip labeled with the name of the center. If no strips are available, he makes another center choice. When the student completes the center, he returns the strip. Eliminating center pileups has never been easier!

Jennifer P. Gann
Seymour Primary School, Seymour, TN

Center Supply Pictures

Post a picture-supply list at each of your centers to help children independently prepare for centers. Gather pictures of items that are used frequently in your classroom centers, such as glue, scissors, and crayons. Cut out and laminate each picture. Each day post the pictures of the supplies needed at each center. Have students check for, then gather, the needed supplies for their assigned centers.

Mary Langford, St. Agnes School, Butler, WI

In the Center

This management technique helps keep your center time running smoothly. Label a nametag for each child and laminate it. Attach the loop side of a Velcro sticker to the back of each nametag. In each center, attach the hoop side of as many Velcro stickers as you will allow children in that center at a time. To select a center, each child attaches his nametag to a Velcro sticker in the center of his choice. To change centers, he simply removes his nametag and attaches it to a Velcro sticker in the new center. This method will allow children to change centers freely, while controlling the number of children in each center at one time.

Monica Severt
Maysville Elementary School
Maysville, NC

Color-Coded Centers

Management of center activities is quick and easy with this color-coded system. Post a different-colored construction paper circle at each center, and a smaller corresponding-colored circle on a pegboard. Beside each circle on the board, clip plastic clothespins of the same color to pegs representing the number of students allowed at that center. At center time, encourage each student to select a clothespin and clip it on his shirt. Have him use the center that corresponds to the color of his clothespin. When the student is finished, have him return the clothespin to the center board and select another center.

Terri Smith
Blessed Sacrament School, Trenton, NJ

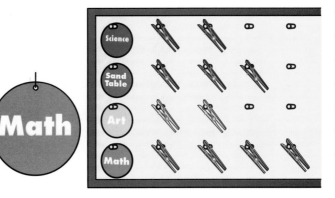

Flag Time

Fly a different color of flag at each of your centers to help children choose and change areas with ease. To make a flag, fold a long, rectangular piece of felt in half and stitch around all four sides, stitching about ½ inch from the fold on the folded side. (This will create a casing along the folded side.) Insert a wooden dowel in the casing, and hot-glue the flag in place if necessary. To make a flag stand, drill a hole in a block of wood and insert the flagpole. Place a flag at each center. Attach colored clothespins to each flagpole according to the number of children who may be in that center. When a child enters a center, he takes a clothespin from the flagpole and clips it to his clothing. When he leaves that center, he replaces the clothespin on the flagpole.

Carla J. Moore
Washington District Elementary School, Buckhannon, WV

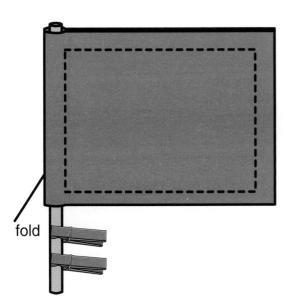

fold

Learning Center Raffle

Your children are sure to use their free time wisely with this learning center incentive. When students complete free-time learning centers, have them write their names on slips of paper and then place the personalized slips in a class raffle box. After a designated number of weeks, draw a name from the box and present a prize to the winning child. Then empty the box and start the activity again.

Lorinda Bodiford, Souder Elementary, Everman, TX

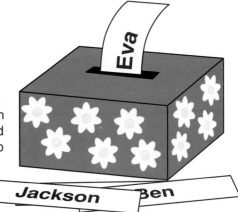

Check Out That Center

This idea will help students remember which classroom centers they have visited. First, label each classroom center with a symbol. Next, give each student a center checklist similar to the one shown. For each center that a student visits, instruct him to put a check mark in the appropriate box. After a student has visited each classroom center, he writes his name and the day of the week on his checklist and then hands it in. You can quickly see if the student has had a chance to visit all the classroom centers; then write a note of encouragement to him.

Sandy Shaw
Jeannette McKee Elementary
Jeannette, PA

Center Cards

Use these center cards if you'd like to be sure that each child in your class visits all your centers. To make a center card, divide a sheet of paper into as many sections as you have centers, plus a name space. In each section, write the name of a different center and add a visual cue such as a drawing or glued-on picture. Keeping a master copy, duplicate the card for each child. Punch a hole at the top of each card, add a paper reinforcer, and attach a short loop of yarn for hanging. When a child has finished working in one center, have him color that center's picture on his card. Encourage youngsters to have each section colored by the end of the week. At the beginning of the next week, give each child a new center card and continue in the same manner.

Marion Mobley
Redcliffe Elementary, Aiken, SC

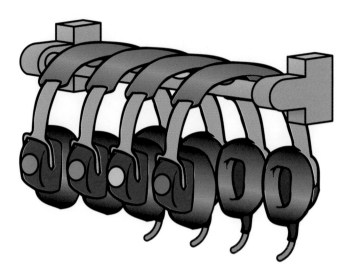

No More Tangles

This organizational tip keeps your youngsters from becoming all tangled up in your listening center. Mount a sturdy, plastic towel bar on the wall nearest your listening center. Using colored markers or adhesive dots, clearly label the headsets and the towel bar with corresponding colors. Then label the outlets at the listening center with the same color code. A student identifies the color-coded outlet that is nearest him and removes the matching headset from the bar. At the end of the activity, he returns the headset to its appropriate location.

Melana Watley
Britt David Elementary, Columbus, GA

Reproducible Gameboards

Here's a nifty way to turn a reproducible gameboard into a kid-pleasing center activity. Color the gameboard and then glue it inside a clean and empty pizza box. (For added durability, cover the gameboard with a layer of clear Con-Tact covering.) Store any required game pieces—such as a spinner, dice, or game markers—inside the box. Invite a student or two to decorate the box according to the game's theme. The box increases the appeal of the game, makes the game easy to store, and provides a quiet surface for rolling dice.

Hope Harbin, Hephzibah Elementary, Hephzibah, GA

Shapes Mark the Spot

Too many youngsters at the sand or water table? Try this simple solution to overcrowding. From sheets of colored construction paper, cut large shapes to correspond to the number of children desired at the table. Cover each shape with clear Con-Tact covering. Tape the shapes securely to the floor around the table. As a student selects the sand or water table activity, have him stand on a shape. When every shape is occupied, encourage other students to choose alternate activities until a shape at the table becomes available.

Lisa Vik
Austin Elementary
Vermillion, SD

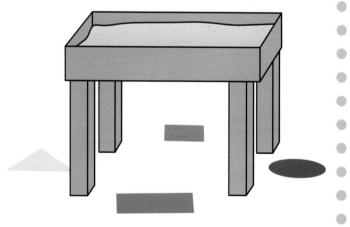

Musical Button

Signal to youngsters when center time is over and it's time to move quietly to the next activity. Purchase a musical button (the kind that is sometimes sewn in a doll) from a craft store. Tell students that each day when center time is over, the musical button will sound. On this cue, have students move quietly into position for their next activity. Choose a student who cleaned his center quietly, and write his name on the board. This student will have the honor of pushing the button after center time the next day.

Connie Crocker
Goose Creek School District, Baytown, TX

Cleanup Captains

Do you spend more time than you'd like transitioning from center time to the next activity? Here's a tip to ease your load and put the children in charge! After signaling students to begin cleaning up, select a hardworking child from each center to be the captain. Have her inspect the center and dismiss her group to the next activity when she thinks the center is neat and tidy. Remind students that if the captain excuses a group with a messy center, *the captain* must finish the work herself. Aye, aye, captain—these centers are shipshape!

Ginni Turoff
China Grove Elementary, Kannapolis, NC

Silent Signal

Monitoring independent workers just got easier! For each student, laminate a red poster board flag like the one shown and use a Velcro fastener to attach it horizontally to the side of his desk. When a youngster needs assistance, he alerts you by turning his flag upright. Now there's an idea that really delivers!

Michele Curlings
Oak Grove Elementary School, Lexington, SC

Signal System

Cooperative learning is a great teaching strategy, but it can be difficult to monitor each group and determine who needs your help. To check the status of the groups at a glance, give each group a laminated circle that is red on one side and green on the other. When a group is working successfully, it displays the green side of its circle signaling that the group is "on the go" with its assignment. When a group needs assistance, it displays the red side of its circle to show that the group has "come to a stop." A quick glance around the room will reveal any group that needs your attention.

Linda Lovelace, Halifax Elementary School, Halifax, VA

Red Light/Green Light Necklace

Do your little ones interrupt when you're working with other children? If so, don a red light/green light necklace. To make a necklace, cut one red and one green construction paper rectangle that are identical in size. Glue the rectangles back-to-back; then laminate them. Punch a hole near one end of the rectangle. Insert yarn through the hole and tie the yarn to make a necklace. Explain to students that the green side represents a green light. When it shows, they can approach you for help. The red side represents a red light. When it shows, students must wait until later to ask for help. Use this easy management system as a helpful reminder for your little ones.

Michele Garza, Whitney Elementary, Whitney, TX

Cluster Buster

Do your students cluster around your desk as they wait to consult with you? Try this! Ask youngsters to organize themselves as if they were standing in line at the checkout counter of a local store. Explain that this is how you would like for them to line up at your desk. The next time students begin to cluster, ask them to get in checkout formation. It works like a charm!

Deanna Whitford, Holt Elementary, Holt, MO

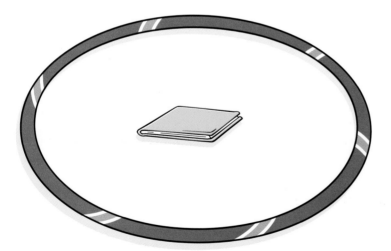

Magic Circle

Use a plastic hoop as a magic circle to establish a one-on-one working relationship with individual students. During your youngsters' free-time activities, place the hoop on a rug; then sit inside the magic circle with a designated student. Use this time to review a specific skill, read aloud a book, or chat with your student. Choose a different child each day for the magic circle. Your little ones will love the idea of receiving such special attention.

Stephanie Larson
Iola, KS

Now Hear This!

With this idea you can quietly capture the attention of students actively engaged in conversational activities. Simply whisper a direction for students to follow, such as "If you can hear me, touch your ear," or "If you can hear me, raise your hand." As youngsters begin to notice their classmates following your directions, they will tune in to find out what you are saying. Before you know it, your entire class will be all ears.

Beth Bill
Prospect Elementary
Lake Mills, WI

Noise Level

To help your class keep the noise level down when working in groups, use this chart. Cue your class to what you expect the noise level to be by pointing to the appropriate picture on the chart. This will indicate to your youngsters how loud or soft their conversations should be. So whether the noise level should be as quiet as a mouse or roaring like a dragon, this chart is sure to be helpful.

Becky Wheeler
Woods Cross Elementary
Woods Cross, UT

Lesson Helps

Quiet Mouse Game

When it's necessary to speak with a visitor while your students are present, engage them in this quiet game. To begin play, choose one student to be a Quiet Mouse. This child stands silently at the front of the room and looks for other quiet students. As soon as the Quiet Mouse points to another quiet student, the two students trade places. The new Quiet Mouse then searches for his replacement. The game continues in this manner until the visitor leaves the room.

Carol Woodham
Seminole Primary
Donalsonville, GA

Colorful Reminders

Colorful apple cutouts are just what you need to monitor classroom noise. Post a red apple to signal a quiet work time. Post a yellow apple when a moderate level of noise is acceptable. If any noise level is okay, post a green apple. Students respond to the colorful cues, and that means you'll receive a bushel of cooperation!

Janica Peppard
Pine Tree Academy
Freeport, ME

Specials of the Day

These handy reminders guard against forgetfulness! Label one poster board rectangle for each day of the school week. On each resulting poster, list the names and times of the specially scheduled classes your youngsters attend during that day. Keep all five posters on display at once, or put a class helper in charge of displaying the appropriate daily poster. Substitute teachers also find the posters especially helpful.

Sue Fichter
St. Mary School
Des Plaines, IL

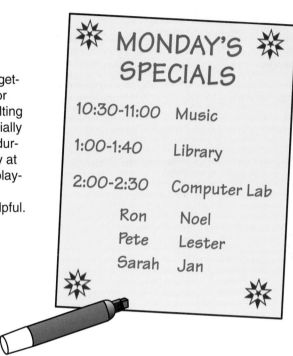

So Simple to Tell!

Have you ever had a child create a painting masterpiece only to find that there was no space left for his name? Here's a simple solution. Have the child write his name on the art paper *first*. Then he simply turns the paper over to paint. With this method, there's no need to find a way to label the wet-paint page!

Carol Beegle
Cen-Clear Child Services, Inc./Head Start
DuBois, PA

Passing the Magnets

Determining which children collect the completed assignments at the end of an activity is a cinch using this simple system. To begin, attach a decorative magnet to one desk in each row or group. The children who have magnets attached to their desks collect the assignments at hand. After placing the assignments in a designated location, each helper removes the magnet from his desk and attaches it to the desk of another student in his row or group. (In advance, establish a predetermined route for passing the magnet in each row or group.) The next time an assignment needs to be collected, these youngsters will be in charge. Students continue passing the magnets in this manner day after day. It's fun, and it's fair!

Brenda King, Reed Elementary, Georgetown, OH

Collecting Student Work

Reinforce your youngsters' alphabetizing skills and save yourself precious minutes with this collection tip. Instead of randomly collecting completed work, have an alphabetical pickup. To do this, have students bring their papers to you in alphabetical order. After you've graded the papers, you can quickly transfer the students' scores into your alphabetized grade book. And if you file your youngsters' work in alphabetized student folders, filing the papers is also a snap!

Catherine L. Nelson, Edisto Primary School, Cordova, SC

Room 104
Ada
Barry
Breyanna
Cathy
Clevell
Diane
Donna
Dwight
Jackson
Matthew
Pam
Rob
Sheila
Steven
Warren

Student Checklists

A supply of student checklists can save you time in a variety of ways! Use a checklist to determine which students have not turned in a homework assignment or still need to return a permission form. Keep track of parent communications on a student checklist, or monitor which students have received positive notes from you during the month. You can also place a checklist at a center and ask students to cross off their names as they complete the center activity. The possibilities are endless!

Susan Sawyer, Hickory Elementary, Bel Air, MD

Silent Echoes

Wish you could keep a lid on echoed responses like "That was my answer!" and "I was going to say that too!" without discouraging student participation? Here's the perfect solution! Show students how to sign the phrase "Me too" in sign language. This is done by signing the letter *y* (see inset), and then, with your palm facing down and your thumb pointed toward your chest, moving your hand back and forth horizontally as shown. When you see students signing "Me too," acknowledge their response with a phrase like "I see several of you agree with Matthew." You'll have plenty of student participation and minimal interruptions.

Cheryl Phillips
Baltimore, MD

Magic Words

If your students spring into action before you complete oral instructions, consider using magic words. Each morning announce a magic-word category such as cereals or vegetables. Before delivering oral instructions, tell students to remain still and listen carefully until they hear a magic word. After completing your instructions, call a word from the category of the day. Students may follow the given instructions once the word has been called. Keep students on their toes by occasionally calling words from inappropriate categories!

Susan Keith, Fairview Elementary School, St. Louis, MO

Hand-Raising Help

If you're constantly reminding students to raise their hands, try this! At the front of the classroom, display a large laminated grid that has 100 or more blank spaces. Each time students remember to raise their hands, use a wipe-off marker to color or check off one space on the grid. When the grid is full, present the class with a predetermined reward. Then wipe the grid clean and use it to reinforce another positive behavior!

Christy Reichard, Campbell Elementary School
Springfield, MO

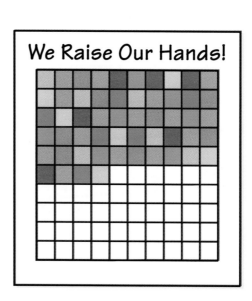

We Raise Our Hands!

Marked for Success

Do you find that your students have a difficult time locating pages in their textbooks? If so, this timesaving tip is for you. Make a set of personalized, construction paper bookmarks for each student. Laminate the bookmarks for durability; then distribute them to students. When a lesson is over, ask students to use their bookmarks to mark the page. The next time that textbook is used, have the child open to the marked page and you're ready to begin a new lesson! For each textbook used, have students repeat this process using a different bookmark from their sets. Keep enthusiasm for this activity high by periodically rewarding students who have their bookmarks on the correct page.

Phil Forsythe
Northeastern Elementary School
Bellefontaine, OH

The Silent Check

Save precious teaching time by keeping class reminders to a minimum. List frequent reminders on the chalkboard, such as "Name on paper," "Desk clear," "Feet on floor," and "Ready to listen." Then begin activities with a silent check. Read aloud the expectations that apply, pausing after each one. If a student has fulfilled it, he makes a large check mark in the air. Students are so eager to "check off" their positive behaviors that they complete each reminder on the spot!

Lu Brunnemer
Eagle Creek Elementary
Indianapolis, IN

Listening Song

Could you use a new, interactive attention-getting song? If so, here's just the one for you. Sing the song, encouraging children to look at you and sing along, adding motions as they sing.

(sung to the tune of "London Bridge")
I am waiting for eyes and ears,
Eyes and ears,
Eyes and ears.
I am waiting for eyes and ears,
Ready to listen.

Patty Schmitt
St. Patrick's School
Portland, MI

Lesson Plan Updates

Updating and reprogramming your weekly lesson plans is a snap with this slick approach! Create a weekly lesson plan format that suits your needs, and program it with times and classes that remain constant throughout the school year. Laminate the project and post it in an easily accessible location. Each week write your plans in wipe-off marker. As adjustments are needed or lessons are completed, wipe off and reprogram the weekly plan. Just think of the time you'll save!

Stephanie Crawford
Monticello Elementary
Tracy, CA

8:10	Arrival	Table toys, graph
8:20	Circle	Calendar, vegetable kwl
8:45	Centers	
10:15	Recess	Upper playground
10:30	Groups	Reading, math teams
11:00	Lunch	

Here Are the Highlights

If you prepare lesson plans in advance, use a highlighting marker to accent materials that need to be purchased or created. A glance at your plans will remind you what you need to do. What an outstanding tip!

Krista Leemhuis
The Kid's Place
Ottawa, IL

Organization With Punch

Here's a great summer project that will keep you organized! Purchase both a large, three-ring binder and a supply of dividers for each month of the school year. Label a binder for each month; then organize your teaching materials by the month in which they are used. Next, organize each month's worth of teaching materials by subject areas and/or themes and label a set of dividers for each binder. Three-hole punch the materials; then arrange the appropriate dividers and materials in each monthly binder. Now you will be able to quickly locate the materials and ideas that you need for each month of the school year!

Maggie Hucko
Phillis Wheatley Elementary School
Milwaukee, WI

Lesson Plans

Scheduling Tip

Get a clear picture of when individual students attend special classes with this tip. Clip a sheet of clear plastic over each page of your current week's plans and then use a colorful wipe-off pen to program the plastic with desired information. (See the illustration.) Each week transfer the plastic sheet to your current plans and update as needed. A quick glance reveals who is exiting when, as well as when the entire group will be together. A substitute teacher is sure to appreciate this helpful approach.

Darcy Keough
Doolittle School
Cheshire, CT

Here's the Plan

Plan early this year so you can distribute copies of your themes and topics to your students' art, music, computer, and physical education teachers. Knowing what you have planned during the year makes it easy for these teachers to incorporate your chosen themes and topics into their areas of the curriculum. Now that's a schoolwide plan!

Bonnie Kinniff
St. Agatha School
Columbus, OH

*Pizza Craft Idea
Oct./Nov. 1999
Kindergarten
Mailbox
P. 50*

Search No More

Cut down on your search time by using this tip to help organize your monthly planning. When you read through *The Mailbox®* magazine and other teacher resources, keep a pad of sticky notes with you. When you run across an idea that you like, jot down the title, a brief summary, and the resource. Then attach that sticky note to the appropriate month in your planning book. When it's time to plan any given month, your ideas will be right there!

Robyn Carp
The Baldwin School
Bryn Mawr, PA

Fast Find

Have you ever gone to retrieve a unit or idea for your lesson plans that you saw "just yesterday" only to find that you couldn't locate it? These handy tabs will solve that problem. To make a tab, fold a white stick-on label over the top portion of a large paper clip. When you run across a page that you know you'll need in the future, write the topic and the day that you'll need it on the label. Slide the paper clip onto the page and leave it there for your reference.

Rhonda Pearce
Anne Watson Elementary
Bigelow, AR

Highlighting Tip

Have you ever forgotten to bring items from home for a special lesson or activity? Then try this handy tip. When writing your lesson plans, highlight the activities that require you to bring items from home. You can also highlight activities that require extra preparation time. With this system, you'll be better prepared for successful teaching.

Margie Cavender
Wilson Elementary
Crawford, TN

Planning for a Substitute

Making advance plans for a substitute is a snap with this reusable lesson planner. Write or type your daily schedule on a series of large index cards. Where appropriate, leave blank lines for writing specific information. (See illustration.) Laminate the cards. Using a hole puncher, punch a hole in the left-hand corner of each card; then bind the cards together on a metal ring. Using a wipe-off marker, write the lesson plans your substitute will need on the cards. When you return, wipe away the programming and store the lesson planner for future planned absences.

Chris Noel
Monrovia Elementary School
Monrovia, IN

Lesson Plans

Pocket Plans

Display your weekly lesson plans with this convenient chart. On poster board, glue library card pockets in five rows as shown. Label the subjects and the days of the week. Then, on separate index cards, write your daily lesson plans for each subject. Place the cards in the appropriate pockets. To teach a lesson, remove the card from the pocket. All of the information you need is right in your hands.

Denise Johnson
Lundgren School
Topeka, KS

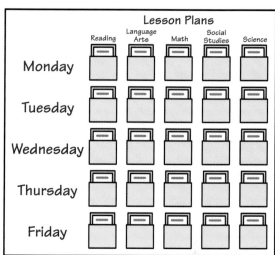

Skill Plan

Use this handy display to keep track of which curriculum skills are being introduced, reinforced, or tested. Visually divide a portion of a classroom wall into four columns. Label the columns from left to right as follows: "New Skills," "Introduced," "Reinforced," and "Tested." Label a cutout for each curriculum skill you are responsible for teaching. Use magnets, adhesive Velcro strips, or masking tape to display the labeled cutouts in the New Skills column; then move the cutouts into the appropriate columns as the skills are being taught. Throughout the year, a quick glance at the display can tell you what skills need attention.

Cindy Sweeney, Homan Elementary School, Schererville, IN

Colorful Reminders

Here's a quick and colorful way to remind yourself about special meetings, appointments, and other important events. For each event for which you want a reminder, write its name and time on a self-adhesive dot. Then peel and stick the preprogrammed dots onto the appropriate spaces in your plan book. Presto! A quick glance at your plan book will remind you of any events scheduled for that school day.

Kristy Osborn
Abraham Lincoln Elementary
Indianapolis, IN

A Perfect Companion!

A user-friendly folder makes a perfect companion to *The Mailbox® Companion®*, the free online service for our magazine subscribers. Label the front cover of a two-pocket file folder for each magazine issue. Organize all materials printed from the Companion inside the folder. Presto! You have more of *The Mailbox®* at your fingertips!

Kelly Mitchell
Van Rensselaer Elementary School
Rensselaer, IN

October/November
Kindergarten–Grade 1
The Mailbox

Have I or Haven't I?

These monthly folders take the guesswork out of knowing which seasonal activities or reproducibles you've used. Label one folder (with two inside pockets) for each month of the school year. Inside each folder, label one pocket "Ideas, Activities, and Worksheets" and one pocket "Used This Month." Slip your seasonal activities into the appropriate pockets; then store the folders in a convenient location. Each month remove the appropriate folder from storage. Throughout the month transfer the activities you use into the pocket labeled "Used This Month." At the end of the month, return the papers to their original pocket and store the folder until next year.

Diane Fortunato
Carteret School
Bloomfield, NJ

Ideas, Activities,
and Worksheets

Used This Month

Library Volunteers

Is it difficult for you to find time to get to your public libraries to gather children's literature? If so, you might like to try this plan that uses classroom parents to help share the load. In advance write a letter asking each parent to plan a trip to the library with his child to check out books for your classroom. Explain that the books that each child brings will be displayed near a sign that reads "Handpicked by [Child's name]!" Add your own details to the letter, such as topics of study, and drop-off and pick-up arrangements. Also include a response form to help you keep track of when new books will be arriving. It's not so hard to keep a full classroom library when you have a little help from your friends!

Carmen Rufa
Bethlehem Children's School
Singerlands, NY

Handpicked by
Jordan

Just-Right Journals

Need a way to brighten up your youngsters' journals? Use napkins! Brightly colored party napkins make lively journal covers. To make a cover, glue a napkin to a large sheet of construction paper; then laminate it. Cut the cover to the desired size; then bind it together with the journal pages. If desired, use seasonal and holiday napkins to make journals that correlate with your current themes. Write on!

Faye M. Barker
Estes Hills Elementary
Chapel Hill, NC

Upside-Down Umbrella

Here's a tip that adds unique display space to your classroom, and it's a great phonics cue too! If you're studying the letter *U* or the weather, or it's simply springtime, hang an open, upside-down umbrella from your ceiling. Tie a different length of yarn to each of the spoke tips. Then tie a large paper clip to the free end of each yarn length. Display student artwork or phonics work by hanging it from the paper clips.

Susan Brown
Southside Elementary
Tuscumbia, AL

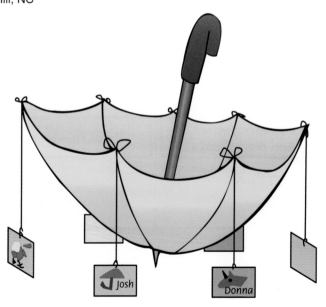

Pocket That Idea!

Need an easy way of organizing art projects, games, songs, and other activities that go along with your favorite books? Inside the back cover of each book, attach a library pocket. Then, on a 3" x 5" index card, write the activities that go along with that particular book. Add more cards to each pocket as necessary. No more searching for those wonderful literature extensions!

Debra Nerko
Parkway Elementary School
East Meadow, NY

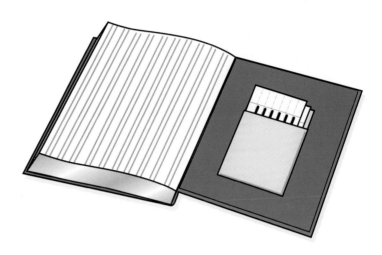

Read It Again!

Use this idea to keep those favorite "read-agains" on hand for just the right moments. Label a box, basket, or gift bag with "Read It Again!" Each time you share a book with your students, take a vote to find out whether or not they would like to read that particular book again sometime. If they vote yes, place the book in the Read-It-Again box. Then, when you need a book at a moment's notice, you'll know just where to look. Substitute teachers will love the Read-It-Again box too!

Jo Ann O'Brien
Lilja Elementary
Newtonville, MA

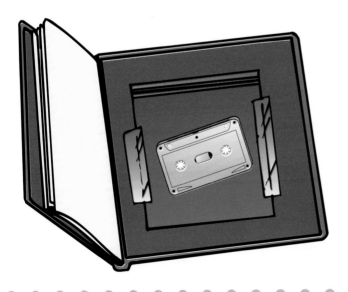

Book and Tape Storage

Are you looking for a way to keep your read-along books and tapes together? Try this simple technique! Use clear mailing tape to attach a Ziploc sandwich bag to the inside back cover of your book. Slide the accompanying cassette inside the bag and zip it closed. Store these book kits in a basket near your listening center. No more searching for a lost tape!

adapted from an idea by Linda Rasmussen
Sparks, NV

"Bin" There, Read That! ✓

Reading will be on the rise with this system for easy student selection and shelving. Program each of several large plastic bins with a different symbol; then fill it with books labeled to match. During reading time, set out several bins and assign a group of students to each one. Invite each child to choose books from her bin to read. When reading time is over, have her return her books to the bin with the matching symbol. Rotate bins and books frequently to provide each child with new reading choices. "Bin" there yet?

Kathleen Miller
Our Lady of Mt. Carmel School
Tenafly, NJ

Literature-Extension Organizer

Do you spend valuable time searching through materials for literature-extension activities? Why not just keep them with the books they accompany? When you receive your latest copy of *The Mailbox*® magazine, cut out or photocopy the literature-extension activities. Then tape each activity inside the front or back cover of your copy of the book. When you want an activity to use with a certain book, it's right there!

Jennifer Travis
Bright Horizons
Randolph, MA

Literature Folders ✓

Keep literature-related activities at your fingertips with this organizational system. Label a file folder for each story you plan to use with your students. When you read an idea that relates to one of the stories, file a copy of it in the appropriate folder. You'll soon have several ideas per title. Writing lesson plans will be a snap, and you'll have a handy resource for substitute teachers.

Margarett Mendenhall
Mary Feeser Elementary School
Elkhart, IN

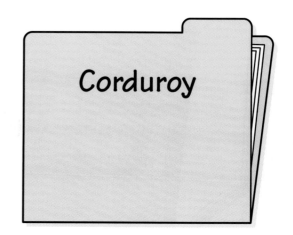

Poem and Flannelboard File

Keep your poems and flannelboard pieces right at your fingertips with this convenient storage system. Each time you use a poem, make a small copy of it to mount on an index card. Place the index card in a labeled envelope with corresponding flannelboard pieces. File the envelopes by theme, season, or holiday in a file box. Your organized poems and flannelboard pieces are readily available whenever you need them.

Liz Mooney
Rayne, LA

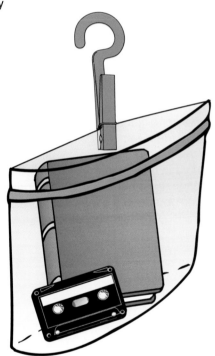

Hook a Book

Taking a few minutes now to organize your book and tape sets will prepare you for fall, plus it encourages this year's students to revisit your collection. Place each book and its corresponding tape in a resealable plastic bag and then clip a clothespin hanger to the bag. Display a sheet of pegboard near your listening center. Insert inexpensive hooks into the pegboard and suspend each bag from a hook. Your students will be all ears!

Alisa T. Daniel
Ben Hill Primary
Fitzgerald, GA

Durable Bookmarkers

Have you ever wondered how to get your students to return books to the proper places on your class bookshelves? Try using durable bookmarkers! Cut the covers from vinyl notebooks into wide strips. Then write a different child's name on each strip. As a child takes a book from the shelf, instruct him to insert his bookmarker in the book's place. When he returns the book to the shelf, he simply locates his bookmarker and replaces the book as he slides the bookmarker out of place.

Sheryl Spears
Idalia School
Wray, CO

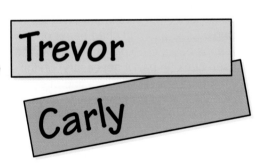

Writers Workshop

Stay informed of where your students are in the writing process with this colorful display. Create and label seven pencil cutouts like the ones shown. Also label a small card for each student. Mount the pencils in sequential order and distribute the student cards. Each child posts her personalized card alongside the pencil that indicates where she is in the writing process. When a student is ready for the next writing stage, she moves her card. A quick glance at the display reveals how the students are progressing and which ones may need assistance during writers workshop.

Carol Kooken
Oakbrook School
Wood Dale, IL

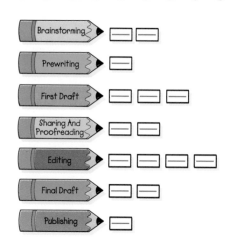

Poetic Organization

Where, oh, where can that poem be? Finding just the right holiday poem or seasonal song is a snap with this organizational tip. In a three-ring binder, place a divider for each month of the school year. Or label file folders in the same manner. Place a copy of each song or poem in the appropriate file. When you need a song to capture the spirit of the season, simply pull one out of the file!

Ericka Lynn Way
Leslie Fox Keyser Elementary
Front Royal, VA

Check It Out!

This hassle-free system will encourage children to share child-made books and other classroom favorites with their parents. Begin by posting a large piece of chart paper on a wall or countertop. To check a book out, a child prints her name, the date, and the title of her chosen book (in part if necessary) on the chart paper. When the book is returned, the child puts a line through the relevant information on the chart. Once a youngster's name is crossed off the list, she is free to check out another book. What an easy way to promote reading, writing, and the home-school connection. Check it out!

Pat Bollinger
Leopold R-3
Leopold, MO

Check It Out!

Michael-Dec 8-Rudolph

~~Kristen-Dec 8-Snowy Day~~

~~Tim-Dec 8-Wake Up Bear~~

Josh-Dec 10-Frederick

Allison-Dec 10-The Night

Word Cards

This idea is a ringer! Mount a cup hook under each letter of your alphabet line. As you study each letter, write words that begin with that letter on cards. When it is time to move on to the next letter, punch a hole in the corner of each of the word cards and place them on a metal ring. Hang the ring of cards on the hook under the appropriate letter. Young writers will be able to use and replace the word cards with ease.

Judy Bingle
Hitchens Elementary
Addyston, OH

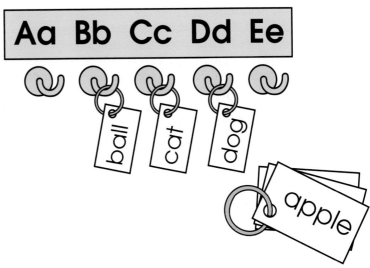

Read-to-Me Library

If you would like to generate reading enthusiasm, then check this out! Employ a read-to-me library in your classroom. To establish this library system, write the title of each classroom book on an individual index card. Glue a library card pocket to the inside cover of each book; then insert the corresponding index card. Give each student a library card pocket to decorate and label with his name. Mount each personalized pocket on a poster board. Hang the poster on a wall near your classroom library. Have each child choose a book he'd like a family member to read to him. Instruct him to take the card out of the book's pocket and place it in his personalized pocket before taking the book home. Upon returning the book, have each child take the card from his personalized pocket and place it back in the book's pocket. This idea not only teaches youngsters responsibility, but it's also a fun way to involve youngsters' family members.

Jeanne N. Taylor
Cincinnati, OH

Big-Book Boxes

Convert a deep big-book box into a convenient storage container for your big books when they are not in use. First, open the center of the box to remove the books; then tape the box together again at the center. Next, seal the bottom of the box with tape. Trim off the top flap. Apply Con-Tact covering to the box to improve its appearance and life span. Then slide your big books into the top of the box for quick and easy storage.

Terry Schreiber
Holy Family School
Norwood, NJ

Big-Book Problem?

If you ever have difficulty remembering which big books you have on hand, this idea is for you. You'll need some screws or cup hooks, clear plastic bags designed for hanging big books, and one or more lengths of chain (available from a hardware store) with links large enough to accommodate the plastic bag hangers. Suspend each length of chain from a screw or cup hook screwed into the wall. Also attach the bottom of each chain to the wall, if desired. To display your big-book collection, simply drop each book in a bag, snap it shut, and hook it onto the chain. Then a quick glance reminds you of the big books you have!

Darlyn Haskett
Good Hope School, Frederiksted
St. Croix, U.S. Virgin Islands

Poems To Pass By

If your students become restless waiting for their papers, consider this poetic approach! On a weekly basis, as papers are being dfistributed, have students recite a chosen poem. When several poems have been learned, volunteers can lead their classmates in reciting the poems of their choice.

Judy Covington
Alba Elementary
Coden, AL

A Rainbow of Readers

Most youngsters love to read their creative writings to an audience. There is seldom time, however, for every child to read every day. Here is a great system for helping you ensure that each student will have a chance to read his work aloud by the week's end. When you give a creative-writing assignment, provide five different-colored folders in which students can place their work. Set a limit on the number of papers that can be placed in each folder. Ask students to place their finished work inside one of the folders. Be sure your students understand that if a folder's limit has already been reached, their work must go into a different folder. On each of the next five days, select a different folder and allow the students whose work is inside to read their pieces to you or to the class. After five days have passed, each color will have been chosen.

Brenda Cooksey Gee
Mountain View School
Hays, NC

Garbage Bag Binding

Don't toss those garbage bag ties! Use them to bind your class books. After laminating the pages of each book, punch holes in the pages. Then slip a tie through each hole to form a ring and twist to fasten. Pages can easily be added or removed by untwisting the ties. "Tie-rrific!"

Tricia Cooke
YMCA Kindergarten
Northboro, MA

"Class-y" Books

Here's a smart way to publish students' writing. Stock a view binder with clear sheet protectors. To make a class book, slip your students' writings into the sheet protectors; then slide a student-decorated cover into the binder's clear pocket. Display the publication in your class library for all to enjoy. In addition to being extremely durable, the class book can be used again and again by simply replacing the students' work.

Joan Hodges
Lantern Lane Elementary
Houston, TX

Problem-Solving Solutions

The next time there's a classroom predicament to solve or a holiday party to plan, enlist your youngsters' problem-solving expertise. Post a brief note that requests your students' advice. In the note, ask that each student submit his ideas to you in the form of a friendly letter. With this simple idea, youngsters have an opportunity to polish their letter-writing skills, share their views, and contribute to classroom solutions!

Jan Keer
Irving Pertzsch Elementary School
Onalaska, WI

Story File

Keep your flannelboard pieces right at your fingertips with this convenient storage system. Place a copy of each story and its corresponding felt pieces in a resealable plastic bag. Label each section of a cardboard accordion file with the name of a different story; then place each bag in the corresponding section. Your organized flannelboard pieces will be readily available whenever you need them.

Lisa Lieb
Brooklyn Blue Feather Early Learning Center
New York, NY

Book Titles at Your Fingertips

A supply of thematic book titles is right at your fingertips with this tip. When you get books on a given theme from your public library, ask for a printout of the books. As you preview the books, highlight the ones that you like. Then file each printout with its corresponding theme. The next time that theme rolls around, your booklist will be right there.

Helaine Rooney
Georgian Forest Elementary, Silver Spring, MD

Organizing Books and Cassettes

Here's an easy way to organize books and their corresponding tapes. Sequentially number the books; then label each book's tape with a matching number. Store the books on a shelf in order. Sequentially store the cassettes nearby in a tape case. This system is so easy that children can easily locate (and return) the components of book-and-tape sets.

Jeanine Peterson
Bainbridge Elementary
Bainbridge, IN

Literature Activity Folders

Organize your literature activities simply and conveniently with three file folders. Label the front of each folder with the letters of the alphabet. (See the illustration.) File each literature activity by the title of the corresponding book; then write the book title on the front of the appropriate folder. Ideas for future literature lessons will be easy to locate.

Melissa Beasley
North Columbia Elementary
Appling, GA

Blooming Books

Do you wish you had more space to display books in your classroom? A plastic planter box may be just what you need! Set a planter box on a countertop near a window or on the floor beneath your chalkboard ledge; then fill the box with books. If desired, post a sign titled "Blooming Books" nearby. There's a good chance that this new display will sprout a renewed interest in reading too.

Angela T. Sawyer
Burnett Elementary School
Austell, GA

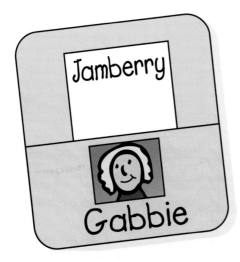

Check Out These Books!

With just a little advance preparation on your part, classroom book checkout can run like a charm! Glue a library pocket inside the back cover of each take-home book. Label a different tagboard card with each book title; then slide each card in the corresponding book's pocket. Next, photocopy a picture of each child in your class. Glue each child's picture to a different library pocket; then personalize the pocket. Arrange all these pockets on a planning chart near the take-home books. When a student is ready to check out a book, he removes the card from the inside back cover; then slides it into his chart pocket. With a simple glance at the chart, each child knows his own book status—and so do you!

Nancy Hopson
Hampton Elementary
Hampton, TN

Sentence-Strip Storage ✓

If you use sentence strips for stories, songs, or games, this storage tip may be just what you need. A plastic water trough used for wallpapering makes a perfect container. The trough is long enough to prevent the strips from curling and bending, and wide enough to hold a number of strips at one time. Attach labeled index tabs to blank strips; then use them as dividers. You'll have all of your sentence strips at your fingertips in perfect condition.

Patricia Landsberg

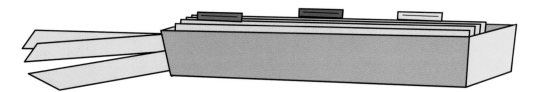

Where's That Pointer When I Need It?

If you're constantly searching for your big-book pointer, try this easy location tip. Cut off a section of a self-sticking Velcro fastener. Stick one side of the tape on the pointer, and the other side on your big-book holder. Each time you are through using your pointer, attach it to the big-book holder. The next time you need it—there it is!

Patt Hall
Babson Park Elementary
Lake Wales, FL

Swap and Check

Use this class activity to reinforce your youngsters' proof-reading skills. Periodically, before students hand in their completed assignments, have them swap papers with their classmates. Instruct the students to proofread their classmates' work and indicate any corrections that need to be made. After a predetermined amount of time, have the papers returned to their owners. Each student then evaluates his paper and makes the needed corrections.

Mary Dinneen
Mountain View School
Bristol, CT

Creative-Writing Organizer

Keep materials for your creative-writing lessons and projects in a handy organizer. Using notebook dividers, separate a large, three-ring binder into sections for the months of the school year. Slide your projects and their accompanying lesson plans and materials into clear plastic sleeves; then file the sleeves in the appropriate sections. Everything you need for successful writing instruction is at your fingertips.

Barbara Fredd
Oregon City, OR

Conference Waiting Area

When children are involved in the editing and publishing stages of a writing project, it is crucial for them to meet with the teacher several times. To reduce interruptions during individual conferences, set up a "Conference Waiting Area." Place four chairs near where student-teacher conferences are held. Students wishing to see the teacher take a seat. If all the seats are full, a student remains at her desk until one of the chairs becomes available. The circle of children waiting for a conference with the teacher will be a thing of the past.

Sandra Lankford
Lancaster Elementary
Orlando, FL

Go "A-head" and Write

Create a quiet environment during independent writing time with an eye-catching hat. When you wear the hat, everyone writes quietly. When you remove the hat, students may ask questions, share their writing with partners, or edit with peers. Now that's using your head!

Shari Abbey
Abilene Elementary
Valley Center, KS

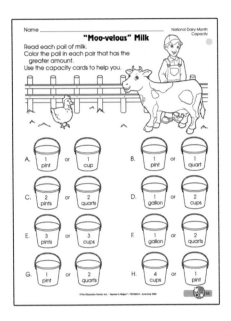

Mastering the Masters

Do your blackline masters get mixed with your multiple copies? Here's a way to keep the original from being misplaced, passed out, or cut up. Using a yellow highlighting marker, color a small dot on the top corner of the blackline master. The bright yellow dot will quickly alert you to set your original copy aside.

Patricia Landsberg
Arminta Street School
North Hollywood, CA

Paper Saver

If you use reproducibles in your workstations, here's a great paper saver. Insert a reproducible in a plastic page protector. When a child works on the page, have him use a wipe-off marker. After the page has been checked, the child simply wipes the slate clean for the next person!

Ruth Meryweather
Child Development Specialist
Uncasville, CT

Favorite Reproducibles

If you're always scrambling to locate your tried-and-true reproducibles, try organizing them with this great tip. You will need a three-ring binder with dividers. Label one divider for each month of the school year. Three-hole-punch your favorite reproducibles (student activities, parent letters, party notices) and place them into the binder according to the month in which they will be used. Your reproducibles will be right at your fingertips when you need them.

Cheryl Sneed
Winters Elementary
Winters, TX

Quick Cards

Save precious time developing theme-related game cards or skill cards. To begin, purchase several small, shaped notepads from educational supply stores. (If you keep your eyes open, you could eventually end up with a notepad for every theme or letter that you study!) Glue each page of each notepad onto tagboard; then cut around the shapes. Laminate the cards; then store them for use. When you're ready to use a certain set of cards, simply program the cards using a permanent marker. To change the skills on a set of cards, wipe off the original programming with a spritz of hairspray and they're good to go again!

Karyn Karr
Cleveland Elementary School
Cedar Rapids, IA

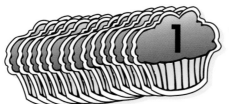
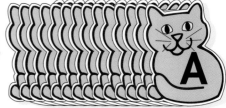

Handy Holders

Do you have students who spend valuable learning time searching their desks for needed supplies? Try this! Use clear packing tape to attach a plastic cup to the side of each child's desk. Suggest that students store frequently used supplies like pencils, erasers, and glue sticks inside. Imagine the minutes that will be saved!

Stacey McKee
Franklin Smith Elementary
Blue Springs, MO

Bingo Bags

Passing out bingo markers is in the bag! For each student, place a supply of bingo markers in a Ziploc bag. When it's time to play bingo, give each student a bag of markers along with a card. When bingo time is over, have each student return his markers to the bag. Collect and store the cards and markers for later use. Now bingo materials can be passed out at a moment's notice.

Drusilla F. Warf
Bluewell Elementary
Bluefield, WV

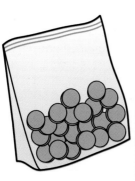

Math-O!				
6	10	22	31	42
5	15	26	33	44
8	16	☺	35	46
2	19	28	36	48
1	20	30	38	50

Pencil Sharpener Cover-Up

Here's an easy way to signal when students may sharpen their pencils. When you don't want students using the pencil sharpener, simply slip an empty, cube-shaped, decorative tissue box over it. Remove the decorative box to signal that pencils may be sharpened. Now that's a sharp idea!

Nancy Y. Karpyk
Broadview Elementary
Weirton, WV

A Sharp Idea

Use one simple device—an electric pencil sharpener—to minimize class-time interruptions. Announce that students may use the electric pencil sharpener before class begins; but once class starts, they may only use the manual sharpener. Children will enjoy using the electric model so much that they'll quickly make a habit of sharpening their pencils before school. It won't be long before you notice the benefit of fewer interruptions.

Pat Hart
C. A. Henning School
Troy, IL

Pencil Sharpener Solution

Here's an easy way to avoid interruptions caused by students sharpening their pencils. Place a container of sharpened pencils and a sign-out sheet near the class sharpener. If a student suddenly finds herself needing to sharpen her pencil at an inappropriate time, she signs one out. Later, during an approved time, she sharpens her pencil and she sharpens and returns the one she borrowed. No more interruptions!

Kim Noviello
JFK Primary Center
New Castle, PA

Material Management

The Borrow Box

If a student has misplaced his pencil, where should he turn? To the borrow box! At the start of the school year, ask each student's family to donate a package of pencils. Sharpen several pencils and use a permanent marker to number each one. Store the numbered pencils in a decorated box and place a notepad nearby. If a student needs to borrow a pencil, he writes his name and the number of the pencil he is borrowing on the notepad. At the end of the day, ask the class helper to make sure that all borrowed pencils have been sharpened and returned. Now there's no need to spend valuable class time searching for missing pencils!

Jennifer Moody
Winship Magnet School
Macon, GA

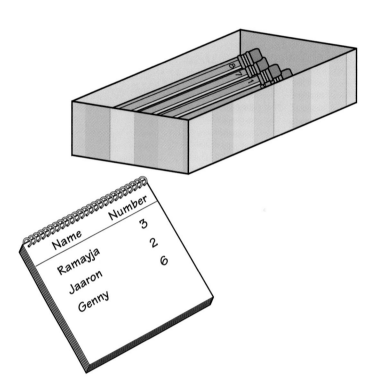

Hold Those Markers!

Try this idea to keep your dry-erase markers at your fingertips. Wrap the hook side of a Velcro fastener around each marker. Then stick a long loop-side of a Velcro fastener to the wall beside your marker board. When the markers are not in use, attach them to the Velcro strip. There you have it—markers everyone can find!

Cassie Hollatz
Lac du Flambeau Grade School
Lac du Flambeau, WI

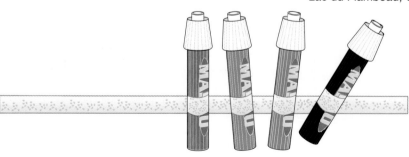

Pencil Bank

Tame the pencil-eating monster in your classroom with a pencil bank. Place a supply of pencils in a special box. When a student needs to borrow a pencil, he takes one from the bank, leaving an item of his own as collateral. When he returns the pencil, he reclaims his possession. No more lost pencils!

Betty Collins

My Space

Here's a quick and simple way to provide each child with his own workspace. Laminate a 12" x 18" sheet of construction paper for each child. Use the sheets when working at tables to prevent glue and crayon marks from getting on the tables. If children are working on the floor, give each child a sheet to help define his personal space when working with manipulatives or to provide a smooth surface when writing and drawing.

Lynn McElreath
Ruth Hill Elementary
Newnan, GA

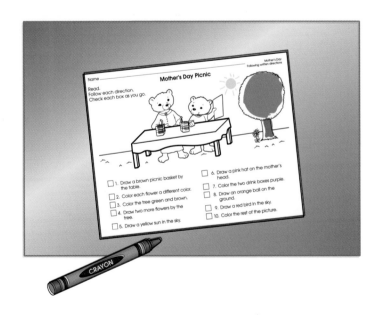

Crayon Lids

Use lids from jumbo crayon boxes to help students keep up with small items. For example, when working with math counters or other small items, have each student manipulate the items in his lid. Lids are also great for holding cut-and-paste pieces until needed. When using a lid in this manner, each student will not only have his own personal workspace, but the lid will also keep small paper pieces in place.

Pablo Millares
Van E. Blanton Elementary
Miami, FL

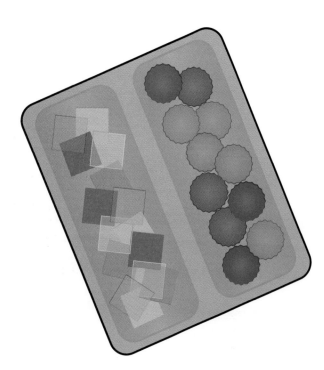

Art Organizer

Keep small art supplies orderly with this neat tip. Collect several plastic cookie and cracker trays that are divided into different compartments. Store craft items such as sequins, pom-poms, and tiny tissue paper scraps in the trays. You'll have easily accessible supplies that are neatly organized!

Martha Bronczek
Bowers Elementary
Massillon, OH

Borrow Until Tomorrow!

Avoid time-consuming delays caused by misplaced school supplies. Place a container of sharpened pencils, scissors, erasers, and glue sticks on your desk. As needed, students borrow items from the container and return them by the following school day. Also keep a stack of request forms near the container so students can alert their parents to their supply needs.

Kristi Gullett
Peoria Christian School
Peoria, IL

Dear Dad,
I had to borrow a glue stick from the Borrow Until Tomorrow container.
I need a new glue stick
Thank you!
Love,
Matthew

Reusable Tubs

Use individual serving–size applesauce tubs to hold individual portions of paint or short crayon stubs. The tubs last well and are just the right size for little fingers.

Jill Beattie, Wilson College Child Care, Chambersburg, PA

Colorful Donations

Do you keep a container of discarded crayons on hand for students to use as needed? If so, then here's a way to replenish your crayon supply for next year's class. On the final day of school, invite students to donate to the class crayon container any used or broken crayons that they do not wish to keep. What a colorful way to reinforce sharing!

Stacie Daley
Queensbury Elementary
Queensbury, NY

Easel Ease

With the use of S-hooks, you can simplify switching sheets of paper on an easel so students can succeed at doing this themselves. First, hang two large S-hooks (available from hardware stores) over the top of the easel. Next, use a hole puncher to make holes in the top left- and right-hand corners of several sheets of art paper. Then slip the papers onto the hooks, and the easel is set up for your young artists. As each child completes her work, she can lift her paper off the hooks, leaving a fresh sheet for the next student. Those S-hooks are simply super!

Suzanne Bell
Fairview Avenue Public School
Dunnville, Ontario, Canada

Just a Squeeze

If your school purchases tempera paint in those big heavy jugs, here's an idea to increase the ease of usability. First, collect a supply of empty sport-drink bottles that have pop-up tops. Using a funnel, pour paint from a large jug into a sport-drink bottle. When you're ready to dispense the paint, simply pop up the top and squeeze!

Debbie Esser
Rome School
Dix, IL

Easy Easel Cleanup

Ask cafeteria workers to save the long boxes that bulk sliced cheese comes in. Put the boxes in your easel trays; then add your paint containers. When the box gets messy, simply toss it out and add a clean one. These cheese boxes are also good for storing folded paper towels or crayons and markers.

Marsha Feffer
Bentley School
Salem, MA

Crayon Canisters

It's easy to recycle sturdy containers into canisters for sorting and storing lost crayons. Cover each of eight same-size containers with a different color of construction paper, representing each of the eight basic colors. Place the canister set in a convenient location. When a child finds a lost crayon, he drops it into the corresponding canister. When a child discovers that a crayon is missing from his box, it's easy for him to quickly take one from a color-coded canister.

Jo Bowman, Caloosa Elementary, Cape Coral, FL

Video Supply Box

Keep art supplies organized and ready to use at a moment's notice by storing individual student sets of supplies in used videocassette boxes. Purchase a class set of used videocassette boxes from a video store. In each box place a sharpened pencil, an eraser, a pair of scissors, a small box of crayons, and a glue stick. If desired, have a class helper sharpen the pencils regularly. The boxes stack neatly on a shelf or windowsill, and you always have supplies ready and waiting for the next project.

Victoria Schirduan
Plantsville, CT

Tabletop Drop Cloths

Protect tabletops from messy paint drips and splatters with this quick solution. Before your youngsters paint, cover each of your tabletops with an old vinyl tablecloth. To clean up, just fold and store the tablecloths. Each time you use a tablecloth, it will collect more colorful paint splotches as it minimizes messes.

Deanna Whitford
Holt Elementary
Kearney, MO

Crafty Carryalls

Turn empty Pringles potato crisps cans into nifty art-supply carryalls! Obtain one Pringles potato crisps can (with a snap-on lid) for each student. Cover each container with colorful Con-Tact paper. Then place inside the container an eight-pack of crayons, a small bottle of glue, a pair of student-size scissors, and other desired art supplies. Have students store their crafty carryalls inside their desks or at another designated location. Now your students' supplies are easily accessible and ready for any project!

Missy Eason and Debra Wingert
Moulton Branch Elementary
Valdosta, GA

Half-Pints of Paint

If your classroom sink is constantly filled with paint cups that need washing, then this tip is for you! Open the top of an empty half-pint milk carton; then fill the carton with paint. Keep the paint fresh for weeks by using a clothespin to close the carton when not in use. When the carton is empty, simply toss it in the trash can. You'll never wash paint cups again!

Carole Tobisch
Denmark Early Childhood Center
Denmark, WI

Simple Drying Racks

When it comes to drying art projects, is there any classroom that has enough space? This drying rack takes up very little room and is easy to make. Simply turn a plastic file organizer on its side. Then cut a piece of cardboard to fit inside each divider. Cover each piece of cardboard with Con-Tact paper. Then slide the covered cardboard pieces onto the dividers to make shelves. These racks are ready to go!

Jackie Wright
Summerhill Children's House
Enid, OK

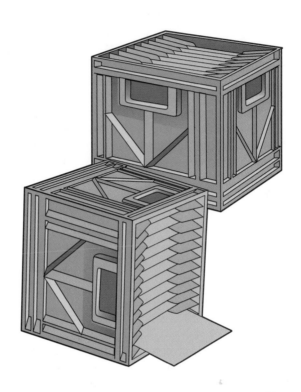

Easy Paint Cleanup

Paint cleanup is a breeze when you "leave it 'til tomorrow." Spoon small amounts of paint onto plastic lids for children's use. Afterward, lay the lids in an out-of-the-way place to dry. The following morning, just tap the lids on the inside edge of a wastebasket, and the leftover paint pops right out!

Marlene Kimmell
Graysville Elementary School
Graysville, IN

Paint-Sponge Cleanup

Empty baskets make paint-sponge cleanup a breeze! After painting, have students rinse the sponges and then drop them in baskets. When you go outside, use clothespins to clip the baskets to a clothesline or tree branch. Let the baskets hang in the breeze until the sponges are dry and ready for painting again.

Amanda K. Haynes
Fountain Inn Elementary
Fountain Inn, SC

Wipe and Wash

When a sink is not conveniently located, the mess created by art projects can be quickly wiped away with this cleanup hint. Keep a container of baby wipes available in the art center. Encourage your children to use the wipes to clean their hands before going to the sink to wash. Also use the wipes to clean the art tables and other surfaces. Cleanup is as simple as wipe and wash.

Gretchen R. Ganfield
McHale Child Care–Preschool
Plymouth, MN

Paint Cup Cleanup

Say goodbye to scrubbing those paint cups clean! Before filling each cup with paint, line it with a plastic sandwich bag. When it is time to clean up, throw the used bag away; then line the cup with a new bag. So simple!

Jean L. Gress
ECC 31
Buffalo, NY

A Tidy Tip

Here's a neat tip that works wonders when youngsters do cut-and-paste activities. Place several damp cloths in each of several plastic margarine containers. Place a container and an empty can on each table. After a cut-and-paste activity, have youngsters place their scrap papers in the cans and then wipe their hands with the wet cloths for easy cleanup.

Adapted from an idea by Jo-Ellen Forrest
St. Louis Public Schools
St. Louis, MO

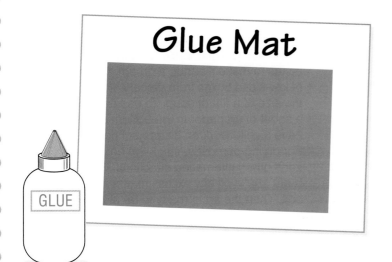

Glue Mat

Glue Mats

Your tables will stay neat and clean with this idea. For each child, glue a large sheet of construction paper atop a sheet of easel paper. Use a permanent marker to program the top of each sheet with "Glue Mat." Laminate the mats. Place the mats on a shelf or in an art center. Have your youngsters use the mats whenever they are using glue. No more messy tables!

Tara K. Moore
Dunwoody, GA

Just a Dot

Teach youngsters this catchy rhyme to help them remember exactly how much glue will do.

Just a dot,
Not a lot,
Only a spot
Of glue
Will do!

Julia Mashburn
Black's Mill Elementary
Dawsonville, GA

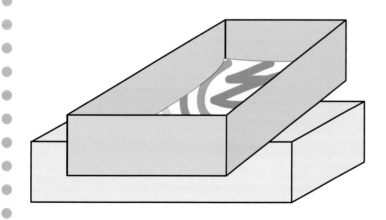

Art Boxes

Do your youngsters like to create art projects with paint, glitter, and glue that sometimes result in a cleanup nightmare? Then try using these art boxes to make cleanup a dream. Gather a supply of low-sided boxes from grocery stores—about the size of a flat of soup. To use an art box, place a sheet of art paper in the bottom of the box and have a child work on his project right in the box. For drying purposes, stack the boxes on top of each other, alternating directions. When a project is dry, shake off any excess matter into the art box. Then the art is ready to be displayed and the excess matter can be collected or tossed out as desired. (To increase the life spans of your art boxes, line them with an adhesive covering.)

Sheila Weinberg
Warren Point School
Fair Lawn, NJ

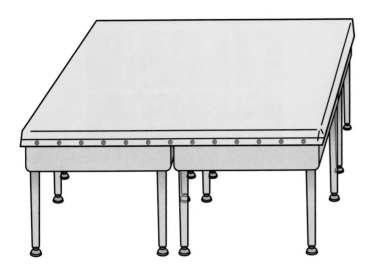

Curtain Calls

If you're about to do a messy project in your classroom, it's time for a curtain call! When you announce, "Curtain call," have students push tables together as you direct them. Then spread one or more shower curtains over the resulting surface. Students can work on top of the curtain while keeping the tables clean. Encore!

Colleen Thompson
Chosen Valley Elementary
Chatfield, MN

Super Shower-Curtain Uses

Showers of uses can come from an inexpensive shower curtain. Tape a shower curtain under your classroom art easel. Paint drips can be easily wiped up with a wet cloth and spray cleaner. If too many messy masterpieces have been created at the easel, machine wash the curtain in cold water.

If students are working together on the floor, have them sit on an additional shower curtain that has been spread in an open space. After students complete their coloring, cutting, or gluing, cleanup time is a breeze. Just wipe and fold!

Tara K. Moore
Hightower Elementary
Doraville, GA

Math

Great Graph!

Make your own class graph with two garbage bags, a wrapping paper tube, and some masking tape! Cut the sides of each garbage bag down to the bottom seam as shown; then tape two of the shorter ends together to make a long strip. Use masking tape to mark the grids on the graph; then tape the top of the graph to the wrapping paper tube. To use the graph, lay it on the floor and have students place manipulatives in the grids. When you are finished, simply roll up the graph around the tube.

Amber Peters
Parkview Elementary
High Point, NC

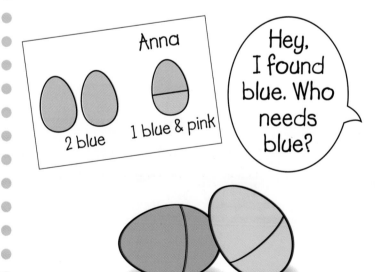

Anna

2 blue   1 blue & pink

Hey, I found blue. Who needs blue?

Happy Hunting, One and All!

Take a crack at this teacher tip that helps egg hunts run smoothly and also nestles in a little reading practice while you're at it. In advance, collect a supply of various colors of plastic eggs. Pack each egg with treats. Then, according to the number of students in your class and the colors in your egg collection, program a card (similar to the one shown) for each child in your class. (These cards serve to regulate the number of eggs each child may find.) For added fun, mix the egg colors! On the day of the hunt, give each child a card and send her hunting! In all the hunting excitement, you'll find your students becoming all for one and one for all!

Martha Alfrey
Southaven, MS

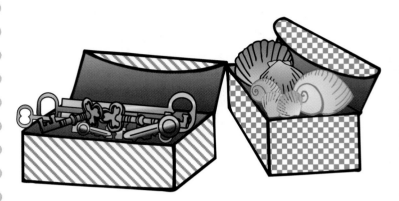

Manipulative Boxes—Supply and Demand

Do you find that you're always in need of more and more manipulatives *and* places to store them? If so, here's a plan that solves those dilemmas! Ask parents to send in empty Velveeta boxes. Cover each box with Con-Tact covering. In addition, give each parent a list of manipulatives that you are collecting, such as keys, silk leaves, seashells, milk-jug lids, etc. As parents send in manipulatives, store them in the covered Velveeta boxes. These boxes stack and store nicely, and they're just the right size for little hands to tote around the classroom.

Mindy Bruce, St. Mark's, Colwich, KS

Math Bags

Do you spend precious minutes of math time distributing and collecting manipulatives? Try this! Personalize a large zippered bag for each child. Every week or so, stock the bags with the manipulatives students need for the next several math lessons. Store the bags in a designated container and distribute them as needed. Or ask each child to store his math bag inside his desk. Every minute saved is one more minute of math instruction!

Kimberly Baker, Skyview Elementary, Richardson, TX

Manipulatives Storage

Use this storage tip to help keep your manipulatives sorted and organized. From an office supply store, purchase several five-drawer office organizers. Label the front of each drawer with the name of its contents and a picture. If desired also label the cabinet and each corresponding drawer in numerical order. To use the manipulatives, have a student remove a drawer. When he's finished using its contents, have him return the drawer to its cabinet. If the cabinet and drawers are numbered, encourage the child to return his drawer to its corresponding place in the cabinet.

Jackie Wright
Summerhill Children's House
Enid, OK

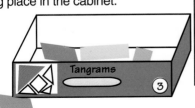

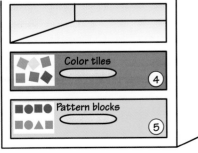

Estimation Chart

Save preparation time with this versatile estimation chart. Leaving the upper one-quarter of a poster board sheet blank, print each child's name and draw a space for writing his estimation. (Leave additional room for the names of children who may enroll later.) Laminate the poster board. When you have an estimation assignment for students, write it near the top of the poster using a transparency pen. Write or have each student write his estimate in the space by his name. When youngsters have compared their estimates with the actual figure, the board may be erased for repeated use.

Kendra Olson
Seneca Elementary School
Seneca, IL

How many olives are in the jar?

Frank _____

Maggie _____

Neil _____

Jerry _____

Two-in-One Shape Up

Here's an idea that will keep your classroom tidy as well as reinforce shape recognition. For each of your student tables, cover a different can (or box) with an adhesive covering. Use permanent markers to draw a different shape on each container (or glue on construction paper shapes). Place a can on each table; then have youngsters store their daily supplies such as crayons and scissors in the can. As you go through the day, designate groups by referring to the shape on the can. For example, you might say, "The triangle table may line up now." In no time at all, children will recognize these shapes—and you will have also kept everyone's supplies in order!

Suzanne Bell Ward
Ancaster, Ontario, Canada

Mini Magnetic Boards

Cook up some magnetic fun with this idea! Use burner covers as individual magnetic boards. Place the covers at a center along with magnetic letters or numbers. Then have students use the letters and numbers on the inside of the cover. If desired, use self-adhesive felt to cover the outside of the burner cover and reduce noise. Now that's a hot idea!

Carolyn Parson
Union Valley School
Hutchinson, KS

Dice Mats

These easy-to-make mats muffle the sounds of rolling dice. To make the mats, cut one-foot squares from nonslip drawer lining. Store the resulting dice mats near your supply of dice. To use a mat, a student presses it flat against his playing surface. Roll 'em!

Marcia Hopkins
James Ellis Elementary
Niles, MI

Puzzle Problem Solver

Do lost puzzle pieces have you puzzled? If so, then here's a tip for you. On newspaper, have youngsters assemble each of your puzzles to be sure that you have all of the pieces. Then flip each puzzle over so that it is facedown. Spray paint the puzzles' bottoms using a different color for each puzzle. After the paint dries, use the puzzles as before. This easy color-coding method will help youngsters see at a glance which puzzle pieces belong together.

Maria Cuellar Munson
Unity Church Preschool
Garland, TX

Puzzle Organizer

Those worn-out puzzle boxes can be the beginnings of *new* puzzle organizers. For each puzzle, cut out the picture from the box top. Code the back of that picture and the back of each piece of that puzzle with the same numeral. Then place the picture and all of the pieces in a large resealable bag that is also labeled with the same numeral. (If you have a pegboard, punch a hole near the top of each bag; then hang each bag on a hook that is labeled with the corresponding numeral.)

Joan Johnson
Elias Howe School
Bridgeport, CT

The Pieces Fit

Keep track of all your puzzles' pieces with this tip. Remove the pieces from a wooden puzzle. Write a number on the back of each puzzle piece and the same number on the back of the puzzle frame. Similarly label your other classroom puzzles, using a different number for each puzzle. When a stray puzzle piece appears, just check the back to see where it belongs. No more puzzling over the pieces!

Robin Souder
Kimball Wiles Elementary
Montevallo, AL

Songbooks

Use this nifty idea to make locating songs, poems, and fingerplays an easy task. Write theme-related songs, poems, and fingerplays on a series of index cards. Laminate the cards. Using a hole puncher, punch two holes at the top of each card; then bind the cards with metal rings to make a book. Provide several blank index cards in each book so you can add to it at a later time. This handy reference will help you find what you need in a hurry.

Jane Walker
Hubbard Elementary
Forsyth, GA

Music Selection

This problem-solving idea will keep your youngsters "humming" to their favorite tunes during music time. To be sure that all students have input on the choice of music selected, take photos or make small pictures that represent some of the students' favorite songs. Insert the photos or pictures in six Ziploc bags and glue them to all of the sides of a small square box. Select a child to toss the box. The photo that lands on top indicates the first song to be sung. Choose a different student each time you need to make a music selection. Photos can be changed as the students' favorite songs change.

Jennifer Strathdee
Parkside School
Solvay, NY

Sing a Song

The magic of music can quiet down any restless group. To quickly settle your class after recess or an exciting activity, choose a song with hand motions to sing three times. The first time the song is sung, ask the class to sing loudly and perform the motions. The second time, direct the class to hum the tune and perform the motions. The third and last time, only perform the motions. Shh...you can hear a pin drop!

Gail E. Joseph-Joireman
Bellingham, WA

Five Little Bats

Neon to the Rescue

Use this glowing idea to make locating seasonal songs and fingerplays an easy task. Program neon-colored index cards with your favorite fingerplays, songs, and poems. Use a different color of neon card for each month or season. For example, use orange cards for October or red cards for February. Keep the cards in an index-file box. This colorful filing system will help you find what you need in a hurry.

Virginia Frehn
Trinity Day Care Preschool
Walnut Bottom, PA

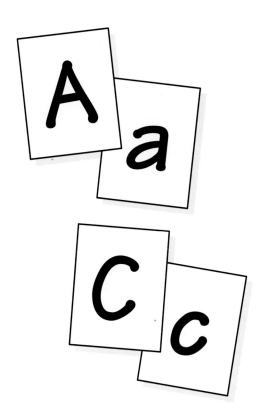

Alphabet Partners

When your students choose partners, are they sometimes just a little bit too choosy? Use this tip to help eliminate hurt feelings and reinforce alphabet recognition. Prepare a set of lowercase alphabet cards and a set of uppercase alphabet cards. To determine partners, give half the class cards from the lowercase set and the other half cards from the uppercase set. (Be sure that each card given out has a mate.) Have students pair up by matching uppercase and lowercase letters. What a pleasant way to pick partners!

Laura Bentley
Captain John Palliser Elementary
Calgary, Alberta, Canada

Picking Partners

Partner cards are perfect for pairing students. To make a set, divide a class supply of blank cards into two equal stacks. Program each card in one stack with a seasonal sticker so that no two cards are the same. Program the second stack of cards to match the first stack. (If you have an uneven number of students, program one wild card.) When it's time for students to pair up, distribute the cards and ask each youngster to quietly find his match. A student with a wild card joins the pair of his choice. Collect and reuse the cards again and again. Easy *and* fun!

Melanie Cleveland
Blackduck Elementary
Blackduck, MN

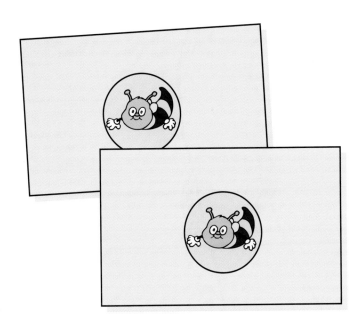

Student Grouping

Color-Coded Assignments

To avoid confusion when making small-group assignments, try this colorful technique. Assign a color name to each small group. When it's time to write group assignments on the chalkboard, use chalk colors that correspond to the group names. If an assignment is intended for the entire class, use white chalk. Learning center assignments can be placed in color-coded envelopes or folders.

Linda Madron
Mary D. Lang Elementary School
Kennett Square, PA

Math - page 18
Science Journals
read a story
printing center

Colorful Student Roles

Pipe-cleaner bracelets are a colorful way to remind students of their assigned roles in cooperative groups. On a sheet of poster board, list each student role followed by a different color word. Post the resulting chart in a prominent classroom location and gather a supply of pipe cleaners in the colors you've listed. When you assign student roles within a cooperative group, give each child the appropriate color of pipe cleaner and have him fashion it into a bracelet to wear through-out the activity. These colorful reminders are sure to promote successful student interaction!

Deb Callan
Bel Air Elementary School
Evans, GA

Friendship Fishbowl

Choosing partners or teams for class activities is fun with this fishy procedure. Cut out a supply of construction paper fish shapes. Personalize one cutout for each student; then place the cutouts in a fishbowl. To create a student group, simply draw the desired number of cutouts from the fishbowl. This method ensures random grouping of youngsters.

Diane Fortunato
Carteret School
Bloomfield, NJ

Pairing Partners

Pair students and develop their vocabulary skills with this seasonal approach. Program a class set of seasonal cutouts with pairs of homonyms, antonyms, or synonyms. To assign partners, distribute the shapes and ask each child to find the classmate who holds the homonym (or antonym or synonym) of his word. Once the students are paired, collect and store the cutouts. Your youngsters' vocabulary skills will quickly take shape!

Janice Keer
Irvin Pertzsch School
Onalaska, WI

Creating Teams

Here's a simple way to divide students into teams or groups. To create four teams, you need four different colors of construction paper. From each color, cut the number of three-inch cards that equals one-fourth of your student enrollment. When it's time to play, randomly distribute the cards to your youngsters and ask students to group themselves by color. Four teams will result in a quick, easy, and colorful manner.

Mary Dinneen
Mountain View School
Bristol, CT

At the Drop of a Circle

Organize your small groups quickly and quietly using this management tip. Assign each group a number; then number a large circle cutout for each group. Laminate the cutouts for durability if desired. When it's time for youngsters to work in their assigned groups, place the circles where you'd like the groups to meet. You'll have a smooth transition into group work and the flexibility to choose the work location that you feel is most appropriate for each group.

Marilyn Haynos
Scranton, PA

Student Motivation and Work Management

Contents

Behavior Modification

Time-Out Assignment

This tip makes the minutes that students spend in time-out more productive. You will need a writing surface and pencils in your designated time-out area. When a child misbehaves and is sent to time-out, give her an assignment sheet like the one shown. Write the date and time, and indicate the number of minutes the child must stay in the area. Then have the student complete the assignment. When her time is up, quickly review her work. The student may leave when her work is approved. If desired, file the assignment for future reference. By rethinking the behaviors that land them in time-out, students are less likely to have repeat occurrences.

Chinita Hodo
Redan Elementary School
Redan, GA

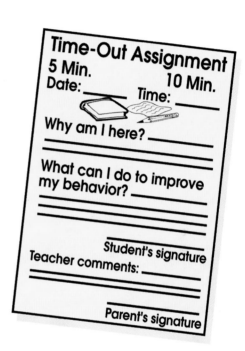

Time-Out Assignment
5 Min.   10 Min.
Date: _____ Time: _____

Why am I here? _____

What can I do to improve my behavior? _____
_____
_____

Student's signature _____
Teacher comments: _____
_____

Parent's signature _____

"Tape" Five!

When a petty dispute arises between students, this approach encourages the youngsters to work out their problem independently. Instruct the students who are involved in the dispute to go to a classroom area where a tape recorder has been set up. Then have the children turn the tape recorder on and talk out their problem. Provide a timer to make sure the students stay within a five-minute time limit. Later in the day, after the students have had a chance to cool off, sit with the youngsters as they listen to their recording. By this time students often realize just how silly their argument was.

Sr. Barbara Flynn
St. Raphael School
Bridgeport, CT

Lunchroom Behavior

Reduce behavior problems in the lunchroom with this positive plan. Personalize a clothespin for each child and then display the clothespins so they are easy for students to retrieve. As each child lines up for lunch he collects his clothespin and clips it to his shirt sleeve. If he returns to the classroom (after lunch) with his clothespin in place, he earns one point for the class. If he is involved in a behavior-related incident and asked to surrender his clothespin, he earns no point. When a set number of class points are earned, reward the class with extra recess time!

Jennifer Norman
Maplewood Elementary
Sunrise, FL

Secret-Agent Numbers

Reinforce problem-solving strategies and minimize interruptions with this management plan. Number a set of secret-agent cards (one per student) and numerically stack the cards on top of your desk. When a student feels that she needs your assistance but you are working with a small group or an individual, she takes a card. Her mission is to answer her question independently or with the help of another available classmate. As time permits, sequentially call the numbers that have been taken from the card stack. Congratulate those youngsters who successfully solved their own cases, and help those students who need your assistance.

Susan Pomfred, Green Meadow School, Maynard, MA

Behavior Modification

Time to Think

Use this behavior plan and turn negative situations into positive learning experiences. Position a "Think About It" desk in a quiet area of the classroom. When a child displays inappropriate behavior, ask her to sit at the "Think About It" desk. Challenge the child to contemplate her behavior and decide what she should have done differently. After a few minutes, meet with the youngster to discuss the situation, determine an appropriate behavior, and, if necessary, agree upon a suitable consequence. This problem-solving approach to behavior management has lasting effects.

Sandra L. Carpenter
Litchfield Elementary School
Litchfield Park, AZ

Think About It

Row 1: ⊞⊞ ||
Row 2: ⊞⊞
Row 3: ⊞⊞ |||

Following Directions Tally

This behavior modification system reinforces following directions. Number each row or table of students; then list the numbers on the board. After delivering oral directions to the whole class, observe each team of students. Draw a tally mark beside the number of each team that followed the directions promptly and appropriately. Continue this procedure for two weeks. Then, as a large-group activity, tally each team's marks. Reward the team that has the most marks with a special privilege or individual treats.

Phyllis Kidder
Okinawa, Japan

Stickin' to It!

Are you looking for a tangible behavior plan for *every* student in your class? Then try this suggestion. Divide each child's daily incentive chart into sections that will allow her to experience success. (Chart divisions will vary from child to child.) After finishing designated time segments, allow children to put stickers inside their boxes. This constant feedback is the ticket to delightful behavior!

Chava Shapiro

	Mon.	Tues.	Wed.	Thurs.	Fri.
Bus		●		●	●
Cubby		●		●	●
Circle	●		●		●
Snack	●			●	●
Center Time				●	●

Positive Puzzles

Reinforce positive behavior with this management idea. To prepare, cut the cover of an unused pizza box into large jigsaw puzzle pieces. Explain to your class that positive behavior will earn them one puzzle piece; then mount each earned piece on a bulletin board. When the puzzle is complete, reward your little ones with a class pizza party. For a variation, laminate and then puzzle-cut the cover of a clean ice-cream carton, popcorn box, or ice pop box. When the puzzle is complete, reward students with the tasty treats from the box.

adapted from an idea by
Tracey Quezada
Presentation of Mary Academy
Hudson, NH

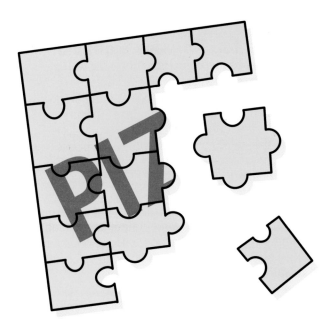

Golden Gloves

Kindness is fostered with this new twist on golden gloves. First, discuss the Golden Rule with your students and ask them to paraphrase its meaning. Then have everyone pretend to put on their golden gloves to help them remember to treat each other with kindness. If, by chance, someone "loses" his golden gloves, you can gently encourage him to put them back on!

Dee Dee Vetter
Sudley Elementary
Manassas, VA

Points for Positive Behavior

Reinforce positive classroom behavior with this reward system. Enlist your students' help in determining the number of class points that can be earned when the majority of the group displays specific positive behaviors. For example, walking quietly in the hallway might be worth five points and working cooperatively in the classroom worth ten points. If desired, designate points for behaviors that require total class participation, such as perfect attendance. Next, set up a point-keeping system and determine the total number of points the class must earn in order to receive an agreed upon reward. With this system in place, everyone can celebrate the rewards of positive behavior!

Vida Vaitkus, Marvin School, Norwalk, CT

Behavin' Bears

Make good behavior one of the "bear" essentials in your classroom! Create a display, as shown, with the names of all your students. Attach five cutout bears per child to the chart with Velcro fasteners. If a child breaks a class rule, a bear is removed from his or her chart. Specify a consequence for each removed bear. One lost bear may mean time-out. A fifth lost bear may mean a call to a parent. At the end of each day, reward students who have kept all of their bears with "hug notes" to take home to parents. Parents are encouraged to discuss lost bears. And, of course, they get to give plenty of bear hugs! Replace the bears so every child begins a new day with five bears.

Lisa Freeman-Cash
Chester A. Moore Elementary School
Ft. Pierce, FL

We're Growing...Growing...

With this cute little guy around, good behavior will be growing by leaps and bounds! Begin by cutting out a designated number of construction paper circles (20, for example). Decorate one circle to resemble the face of a caterpillar and mount that circle on a wall. Add construction paper feet to the remaining circles. Tell your class that each time they demonstrate positive behavior, you will mount a circle behind the caterpillar face. When the caterpillar reaches a length of 20 circles, everyone will celebrate. (To heighten the anticipation for younger children, you might like to put a piece of tape on the wall to indicate what will be the finished length of the caterpillar.)

Virginia Chaverri, Costa Rica, Central America

Lottery Can

Encourage good behavior with a lottery can. Cover an empty coffee can with Con-Tact paper. Cut a supply of one-inch strips from old worksheets or other discarded papers. Each time you spot a youngster displaying good behavior, reward him with a strip. Have the youngster personalize the strip and deposit it in the lottery can. At the end of the day, draw out several names and present each winner with a special reward. Youngsters will soon see that the better their behavior, the better their chances of winning.

Betty Collins, Van Buren Elementary, Hamilton, OH

Good Behavior Is Not Extinct!

If you have a dinosaur theme in your classroom, here's an idea to promote good behavior. First, glue a classroom quantity of library pockets on tagboard. After writing each child's name on a different dinosaur cutout, glue cutouts to the pockets; then laminate the board. Run a razor blade along the opening of each pocket to reopen the library pockets. As a class, decide on your classroom rules and create a legend. Then cut a supply of the needed colors of construction paper strips. Mount the title and a dinosaur cutout on a wall. When you see a child displaying good behavior, just slip one of the colored strips into his pocket on the chart. Each day reward children as you see fit. Good behavior will be roaming your classroom as children try to get all the colors in their pockets.

adapted from an idea by Stacy L. Fritz
Gilbertsville Elementary, Gilbertsville, PA

We the people of Ms. Fitz's class, do hereby agree to follow these classroom rules:
1. Be kind.
2. Follow Directions.
3. Keep hands and feet to yourself.

-excellent day
-super day
-great day
-good day

COMPLIMENT CHAIN

Compliment Chain

Recognize and reward your students' outstanding behavior with a compliment chain. Keep a supply of construction paper strips handy. Each time your class receives a behavior-related compliment from a staff member, parent volunteer, or other adult, add a link to the chain. When a predetermined number of links is earned, reward students with a popcorn party or another desired treat or privilege.

Jennifer Norman
Maplewood Elementary
Ocala, FL

The Code Word for Quiet Is...

To help foster ownership of classroom management, engage students in a discussion to choose a monthly code word (or phrase) that will signal them to quiet down. For example, during August you might decide to use the phrase "Listen for the school bus." When you say this phrase, students know to be quiet and listen. Other examples include "Listen for the apples dropping" (September), "Listen for the Great Pumpkin" (October), and "Listen for the reindeer" (December).

Diane Martin
Grace Edgett Child Development Center
Erlanger, KY

Reward Puzzle

All the pieces will fit together when you use this motivating reward system. Place a wooden puzzle frame without its pieces (12 pieces or less) on a table in the front of your room. Set the puzzle pieces next to the puzzle. Each time you catch a student doing something nice for someone else or you notice your class as a whole making an outstanding effort, add a puzzle piece to the puzzle. When the puzzle is completed, reward your little ones with a treat party.

Wilma Droegemueller
Zion Lutheran School
Mt. Pulaski, IL

Good Behavior

Good Behavior Bonus

An element of chance adds to the appeal of this weekly behavior reward! Survey students to discover the kinds of rewards they find most appealing. Then write several suggested rewards (like "ten minutes of extra recess" or "watch a book-related video") on individual paper slips. Place the strips in a gift bag. Tell the class that each Friday every student who displayed outstanding classroom behavior throughout the week earns a good behavior bonus. Explain that the bonus will be drawn from the bag of student-suggested rewards on Thursday afternoon (giving you time to prepare) and presented on Friday afternoon. Outstanding classroom behavior is in the bag!

Linnae Nicholas
Cuba Elementary School
Cuba, NY

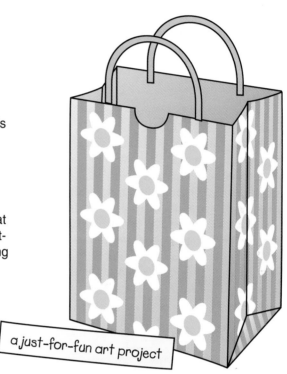

a just-for-fun art project

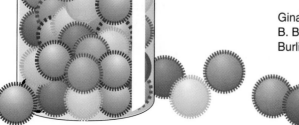

Collecting Class Compliments

Reinforce positive student behavior with this one-of-a-kind idea. All you need is a clean, empty container and a supply of pom-poms. Each time the class receives a compliment from you or another staff member, drop a pom-pom into the container. When the container is half-full, present each student with a sticker or another small reward; when it's completely filled, plan a class party. You can count on this incentive to keep end-of-the-year behavior in line!

Gina Marinelli
B. Bernice Young Elementary School
Burlington, NJ

Compliments Chain

To increase your students' good behavior and build their self-esteem, try this positive approach to discipline. Copy the poem below onto a desired tagboard shape; then use an X-acto knife to slit the lower edge of the cutout as shown. (The slit should be approximately two inches in length.) To start your chain of compliments, insert a construction paper strip through the slit; then glue the ends of the strip together. Prominently suspend the resulting display from your classroom ceiling. Each time your students receive a compliment from a member of the school staff, a parent volunteer, or another visiting adult, attach a link to the chain. When the chain reaches the floor, reward your students as desired.

Peggy Smith
Skyland Elementary
Lyman, SC

For all the nice things people say,
We'll add another link today.
And when the chain and floor do meet,
Ms. Smith will bring us a treat.

Three Minutes of Silence

Take three—three minutes of silence that is! Whenever youngsters need a few minutes to settle down or you need a few minutes of peace and quiet, simply turn over a three-minute egg timer and say, "Three minutes, please." This phrase is youngsters' signal to sit quietly and watch the grains of sand fall through the timer. You'll be amazed just how much difference three minutes of silence can make!

Cherry Hester, Presbyterian School, Jonesboro, AR

Good Behavior

Brag Tags

Here's an inexpensive way for you to brag on your students and build their self-esteem. Begin by collecting a file of cute clip art. When you have a good supply, cut out the pictures; then arrange and glue as many as possible on a sheet of paper. Write a positive comment on each picture; then make a supply of the whole page. Color and cut out the pictures; then laminate them if desired. Store these brag tags in a handy place. When you'd like to recognize a student, simply reach for a brag tag, attach a loop of masking tape to the back, and pat it on!

Note: To keep your brag tags in stock and also reinforce the home-school connection, ask parent volunteers to help color the copies or cut out laminated pictures.

Norma Stotts
Jonesboro Kindergarten Center
Jonesboro, AR

Special Assistant ✓

Promote positive classroom behaviors with a daily-assistant program. Each day watch for an undisclosed behavior. At the end of the day, reveal the behavior, report sightings of it, and select a child who repeatedly displayed it to be your special assistant the following day. Make an effort to reward each child's positive behaviors before the end of the year. Happy students, great behavior, and a little extra help for the teacher—that's a Grade A plan!

Pam Rawls, Harpeth Valley School, Nashville, TN

Sunshine Basket

Show students that their good behavior brightens your day! Place a small basket within easy student reach. Each time you observe a student displaying exemplary behavior, ask her to personalize a small sun cutout and then drop it in the basket. At the end of each week, draw several names from the basket and reward each of these students with a small treat or happy note. Then empty the basket and you're ready to reinforce positive behavior the following week. Let the sun shine in!

Gina Marinelli
Bernice Young Elementary
Burlington, NJ

Stretch Toward Good Behavior

Help your youngsters stretch toward perfect hallway behavior with this fun-filled idea. Cut out a tall giraffe shape from yellow paper and 20 giraffe spots from brown paper. Add facial features and other desired details to the giraffe; then laminate the cutout and the spots. Display the giraffe in an accessible classroom area and store the spots nearby. Each time the class shows exceptional hallway behavior, have a student tape a spot on the giraffe. Reward the class with a special treat or privilege when all 20 spots are in place. What a gigantic way to encourage positive hallway behavior!

Leann Schwartz, Ossian Elementary School, Ossian, IN

Good Behavior Tickets

Cite positive behaviors with tickets—raffle tickets, that is! Cut a supply of construction paper tickets or use tickets from a preprinted roll. Each time a student demonstrates a positive behavior, award him a ticket. Have students personalize their tickets before dropping them into a designated container. Periodically draw a ticket from the container and award its owner a special prize or privilege. "And the winner is..."

Cathy Cavasos, Hickok School, Ulysses, KS

Building Self-Esteem

Increase a student's self-esteem by sending her to the principal's office? You bet! You will need the approval of your school principal and a supply of stickers (computer-generated or specially ordered) that read "I Visited the Principal! Ask Me About It!" When a student demonstrates exemplary behavior or academic success, press a sticker on her clothing and send her to see the principal. The principal then spends a few moments speaking with the child about her success. When the student returns to the classroom, she'll be grinning from ear to ear!

Roxanne Ward
Greenwood Elementary School
Sylvania, OH

I Visited the Principal!
Ask Me About It!

I Visited the Principal!
Ask Me About It!

Good Behavior

Good Behavior Bulletin Board

Ahoy, mateys! Here's the key to great student behavior! Program a paper strip with the title "The Key to the Treasure Is Good Behavior!"; then staple the paper near the top of a bulletin board. Use a pushpin to suspend a key cutout below the first letter in the title. Staple a decorated treasure chest cutout to the right of the paper strip. Tuck a small card labeled with a class reward or privilege behind the treasure chest. Each time that the class exhibits exemplary behavior throughout the day, move the key to the right one letter. Continue in this manner until the key reaches the treasure chest. Then remove the card and reveal what treasure the students have earned. No doubt your youngsters will do their best to be as good as gold!

Fran Rizzo
Brookdale School
Bloomfield, NJ

The Key to the Treasure Is Good Behavior!

Behavior Incentive

Encourage positive student behavior with an easy-to-manage incentive. Think of an incentive in the form of a sentence, such as "An extra recess sure would be nice!" Then, on the chalkboard, draw a series of blanks to represent each word in the sentence—one blank per letter. Each time you observe students exhibiting a positive classroom behavior, write a letter in one blank. When all the blanks are filled and the incentive is revealed, reward the students accordingly. You can count on students trying to guess the class reward as they practice positive classroom behaviors!

Sandy Wiele
Peoria Christian School
Peoria, IL

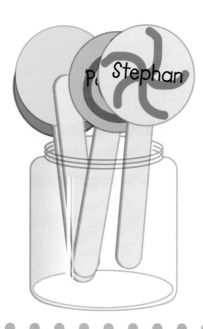

Stephan

Sweet Comments

These lovely lollipops encourage students to recognize their classmates' positive qualities. To make his lollipop, a student personalizes and decorates a four-inch construction paper circle; then he glues the circle near the top of a tongue depressor. Store the lollipops in a plastic jar. Each week gather students in a circle and distribute the lollipops, making sure no child receives his own. Ask each child, in turn, to share with the class something he especially likes about the classmate whose lollipop he is holding. Then collect the lollipops and store them until the following week!

Denise Mason
Port Reading School
Port Reading, NJ

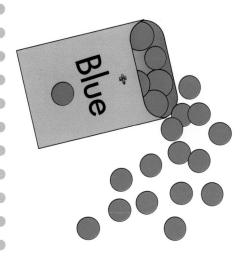

Spotting Good Behavior

Looking for a colorful way to reinforce positive classroom behavior? This idea really hits the spot! Arrange student desks into groups of four or five. Assign each group of students a different color. Label one manila envelope for each group and display the envelopes on a bulletin board or chalk ledge. Also cut out a supply of round construction paper circles (spots) in each designated color. Each time you observe a group exhibiting outstanding classroom behavior, slip a colored spot in its envelope. At the end of the week, let each group count the spots it earned. If desired, reward each group that earns a predetermined number of spots for the week with a special privilege or small individual prizes.

Candi Barwinski
Fleetwood Elementary School
Fleetwood, PA

Good Behavior Coupons

Encourage outstanding student behavior with this weekly incentive program. Label a supply of paper rectangles with a variety of rewards and/or privileges. Place the resulting coupons in a decorated container. At the end of each week, invite every student who has displayed outstanding behavior during the week to draw a coupon from the container. Students can immediately redeem the coupons or save them for later use. In no time at all, you'll have a class of well-behaved coupon collectors!

Ann Southerland, James Bowie Elementary, Midland, TX

Gumball Machine Display

Encourage good behavior with a gumball machine display. Draw a large gumball machine outline on a piece of tagboard. Cut away the circular portion of the design before laminating. Mount the gumball machine on a metal surface. To make gumballs, attach pieces of magnetic tape to the backs of a supply of colorful craft foam circles. Place gumballs in the machine to reward students for positive behaviors. This idea is a sweet way to motivate your youngsters!

Gina Butler-Haslup
Bear Creek Elementary School
Baltimore, MD

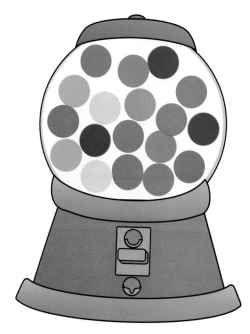

Good Behavior

Crackerjacks

Encourage students to reward their peers with crackerjack awards. When a child is chosen to be a classroom, bathroom, or lunchroom monitor, have him identify classmates displaying exemplary behavior. Then have the monitor report the cracker-jack students to you. Write each crackerjack's name on an award and place the award in a box. At the end of the week, draw one child's award from the box, and present that child with a special prize or privilege. Return the remaining awards to the appropriate children.

Stephanie Miller
Benefield Elementary
Lawrenceville, GA

Thank-You List

Honor students for positive behavior and good citizenship with this satisfying yet inexpensive reward. Write "Thank You" on a section of your chalkboard. As students exhibit notable behavior, write their names on the board. At the end of the day, thank these students with handshakes or hugs.

Kathleen Hunter, Tara Elementary, Forest Park, GA

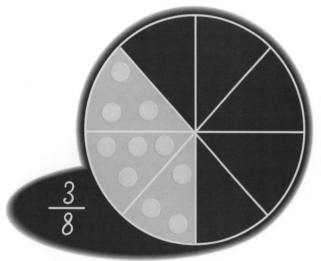

Pizza by the Slice

Reinforce fractions and motivate students to be on their best behavior! Draw a pizza shape on the chalkboard; then divide it into six or more equal slices. Each time you observe exemplary behavior, reward the class by coloring one pizza slice. Also announce the fraction that tells how much pizza is colored and write it near the pie. When the entire pizza is decorated, reward the class with a tasty snack of pizza-flavored Goldfish crackers. Then erase the toppings, reslice the pizza, and repeat the process. Yum!

Dawn Scott
Baxter Elementary
Midlothian, TX

Roll Out the Red Carpet

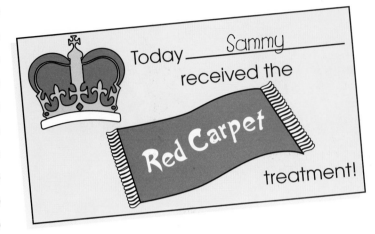

Students feel like royalty when they receive the red-carpet treatment for personal successes. Place a square of red carpet underneath the desk of each student who demonstrated outstanding behavior or academic progress the previous school day. Present each student with a red certificate that entitles him to a specified number of rewards and/or privileges throughout the day of his reign. Though each student steps down from his throne when the day is done, his positive feelings about himself will have just begun.

Margie Siegel
Wren Hollow Elementary
Ballwin, MO

Private Time

Promote positive student behavior by creating a space in your classroom where youngsters can voluntarily spend a few minutes alone. A chair or a large pillow placed in a classroom nook is all you'll need. Encourage students to visit the area when they need a few minutes to sort through their thoughts and feelings. This unique approach teaches students a positive method for dealing with their emotions, builds self-esteem, and endorses exemplary behavior.

Tina Robertson, Kensington Road School, Glens Falls, NY

Good Behavior Stamp Books

Encourage outstanding student behavior with this easy-to-manage incentive program. You will need some colorful stamp pads, a variety of rubber stamps, and one stamp-collection booklet per child. To make a booklet like the one shown, staple sheets of recycled paper atop a slightly larger sheet of construction paper. Have students display their booklets atop their desks at all times. Each time you observe a student demonstrating positive behavior, stamp the top page of her booklet. When a child earns a predetermined number of stamps, she may exchange the booklet page for a special prize or privilege. For added motivation, occasionally declare "Double-Stamp Day."

Beth Davino
Acreage Pines Elementary
West Palm Beach, FL

Good Behavior

Promoting Good Behavior

Encourage outstanding student behavior with a minimal amount of teacher preparation. Mount an open reproducible (like the one shown) on construction paper; then display the resulting incentive chart in a convenient location. Each time students are observed demonstrating positive behaviors, color a space on the chart. When all of the spaces are colored, reward the students with small individual prizes or a class privilege. If desired, have a drawing to determine which student takes home the colorful chart. Repeat the procedure as frequently as desired.

Kathy Quinlan
Charles E. Bennett Elementary
Green Cove Springs, FL

Flying High!

Good Manners Detective

Enlist your students' help in recognizing and encouraging good manners. Each morning remind students to be on the lookout for good manners. At the end of the day, ask students to recall instances in which their classmates exhibited good manners; then invite one student to tell the class about the good manners that she saw being practiced. Afterward have her announce the names of the students she thought were particularly well-mannered. Thanks to this great idea, your students will soon come to expect from themselves the same good manners they are looking for in each other.

Kathleen Ann Weisenborn
Fricano Elementary School, Lockport, NY

Hallway Behavior

Promote positive hallway behavior with this management tip. First, have each student identify a person that she admires. Explain that whenever the students are walking in the hallway you would like them to imagine that these people are walking right beside them. Discuss the types of behavior that would make these imaginary partners feel proud. Then periodically invite students to tell how these companions have influenced their hallway behavior. For added motivation, have students choose new imaginary partners from time to time.

Anne Esau Ballard
West Homestead Elementary
Homestead, FL

Caught Being Good!

Keep spring fever under wraps with this positive-behavior plan. Keep a supply of paper strips and an eye-catching container on your desk. When you witness positive student behaviors such as being helpful, displaying kindness, and staying on task, note the behavior and the student(s) involved on a paper strip and deposit it in the container. On Friday remove and read aloud the collection of positive behaviors from the week; then tally and record the number of observations on a class graph. Each time the class exceeds its previous best effort, reward students with a popular springtime privilege such as an extra afternoon recess.

Janis Ruf, Navajo Elementary, Albuquerque, NM

Monstrously Good Manners

Looking for a quick-and-easy way to improve classroom manners? Try using monster magnets with your students. To make monster magnets, cut a desired number of circle shapes from a piece of oaktag. Print "Monstrously Good Manners" on each oaktag circle; then decorate each one with a picture of a monster. Laminate the circles for durability; then attach a piece of magnetic tape to the back of each one. When you see a student using good manners, stick a magnet to the metallic portion of his desk. With this incentive, classroom manners will improve in no time at all.

Lisa Dorsey
Heather Glen Elementary
Garland, TX

Good Behavior

Party on Pluto

This out-of-sight motivational plan encourages stellar student behavior! On a bulletin board covered with black paper, mount cutouts of the sun and each of the nine planets. Use a pushpin to attach a spaceship cutout to the sun. Then mount a trail of star cutouts that begins at the sun, ends on Pluto, and connects all the planets in between. Each time the class demonstrates terrific behavior, move the spaceship forward one star. If the spaceship lands on a planet, reward the class with a special privilege such as five minutes of extra recess. When the spaceship lands on Pluto, treat your youngsters to a well-deserved stellar celebration! Far-out!

Jennifer Ellis, Tom Green Elementary, Buda, TX

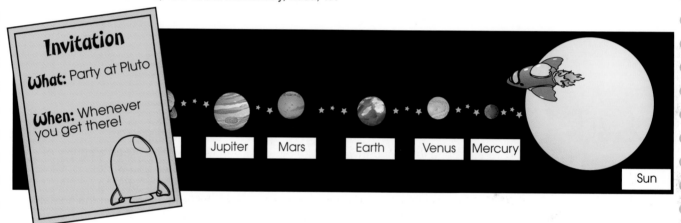

Invitation

What: Party at Pluto

When: Whenever you get there!

Jupiter   Mars   Earth   Venus   Mercury   Sun

Good Egg Incentives

Encourage positive behavior and good work habits with this seasonal approach. Fill a basket with plastic eggs, one per student. Every morning have each student take a plastic egg. Each student attempts to keep his egg until the end of the school day by displaying positive behavior and good work habits. If a student behaves inappropriately, his egg must be returned to the basket. At the end of the day, have those students who have kept their eggs personalize slips of paper; then place the papers and the eggs in the basket. Each Friday afternoon draw one name from the basket. Present the winning student with a special sticker, bookmark, or poster.

Sue Volk
Newton, IL

Cooperative Class

Wrapping up the school year on a cooperative note can be a picnic! Obtain a picnic basket and several items to place inside it, such as plates, utensils, cups, napkins, and a blanket. Display the basket and show students the items you have collected. Explain that at the end of each successful, cooperative school day, one item will be placed in the basket. When all the items are in the basket, the class will celebrate by having a class picnic! No ants allowed!

Holly L. Burkett
Chestnut Ridge School District
Fishertown, PA

The Motivation Station

Keep students motivated during the final month of the school year with a motivation station. Cover a large table with an inexpensive tablecloth; then place a variety of items at the table, such as markers, colored pencils, ink pens, writing paper, notepads, stickers, rubber stamps, and stamp pads. Place two or three chairs at the table and label the area "The Motivation Station." Each day before you dismiss the class, announce the names of students who have been thoughtful and responsible throughout the day. Then make arrangements for each mentioned child to spend 15 to 20 minutes of free time at The Motivation Station the following school day. Keep a record of the students who earn visits to the station so that you can personally encourage youngsters who have not yet earned the privilege.

Ann Marie Stephens, George C. Round Elementary, Manassas, VA

Replenishing Prizes

Here's a nifty way to replenish your supply of inexpensive prizes for next year's class. Invite students to place any unwanted cereal-box toys, giveaways from fast-food restaurants, and other knickknacks in a designated container. Before the start of the new school year, sort through the donations and place the items that are suitable prizes in your classroom prize box.

adapted from an idea by Jill D. Hamilton, Schoeneck Elementary School, Stevens, PA

Good Behavior

Class Pet

A snuggly stuffed animal is a great tool to encourage positive classroom behavior. Introduce your children to their new class pet and allow the children to give the pet a name. Throughout the day, look for students who are following directions, staying on task, or demonstrating positive behavior. Reward those children by placing the stuffed animal on their desks for designated periods of time.

Mary Dinneen
Mountain View School
Bristol, CT

Fill the Fishbowl

Encourage good behavior by having children earn fish to fill up a fishbowl. Place a sign that says "Fantastic Fish" beside a small, clean fishbowl on your desk. When children exhibit appropriate behavior, add candy fish to the bowl. When the fishbowl is full, distribute the candy to the class.

Kathy Klotz, Palmerton, PA

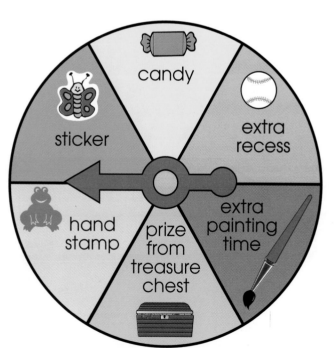

Spin to Win

Add excitement to rewards with a prize wheel. To make a wheel, visually divide a large poster board circle into six equal sections. Program each section with an illustration of a different prize. Attach a metal spinner to the center. When it's time for a youngster to be rewarded, have him spin the spinner to determine his prize. Your youngsters will look forward to receiving rewards even more with this new twist!

Susan Puckett
Pearl Lower Elementary
Pearl, MS

Terrific Tickets

This idea is just the ticket for motivating students to complete their homework on time! Each morning give a raffle ticket to every student who completes her homework assignment. A student writes her name on the back of her ticket and drops it in a designated container. On Friday draw several tickets from the container, and award each selected student a special treat or privilege. Then discard the personalized tickets and repeat the procedure the following week.

Benita Kuhlman
Avon Elementary
Avon, SD

Homework Incentive

This suspenseful reward system makes children excited to turn in their homework assignments. Each day record the names of children who bring in their homework assignments. At the end of each week, place slips of paper labeled with the days of the week into a box; then choose one slip of paper from the box. Students who turned in their homework on the chosen day receive prizes. The prizewinning homework day is always a surprise, so students are eager to turn in their assignments each day.

Jo Ann White
Decker School, Mt. Arlington, NJ

Colorful Homework Chart

Help students keep homework assignments organized with a color-coded homework chart. To create the chart, title a piece of chart paper "Homework"; then write each subject heading in its own color. Laminate and display the resulting chart. When you give a homework assignment, use the appropriate color of wipe-off marker to write the assignment beside its corresponding subject area. After an assignment is collected, wipe the related programming from the chart.

Krista Paciello
St. Catherine-Labouré School
Wheaton, MD

★ Homework ★

Reading:

Math:

Spelling: Study your words!
Test on Friday.

Science: Check your mold experiment. Write an observation in your journal.

Social Studies:

Other:

Homework

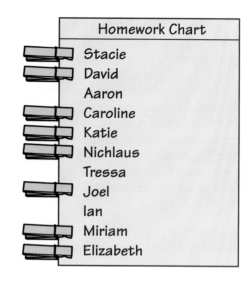

Homework Chart

Stacie
David
Aaron
Caroline
Katie
Nichlaus
Tressa
Joel
Ian
Miriam
Elizabeth

Homework Clip Chart

Keeping track of homework assignments is easy with this handy system. In a prominent area, display a chart labeled with each child's name. Near the chart, place a basket of clothespins. When a child has a homework assignment, he clips a clothespin next to his name. When he returns the assignment, he removes the clothespin from the chart. This system enables you to see at a glance which students have returned their homework assignments.

Marci Godfrey
South Knoll Elementary
Bryan, TX

Homework Excuses

Keeping a personalized record of homework excuses encourages students to turn their homework in on time. In a spiral notebook, personalize one page per student. When a student has an incomplete or forgotten homework assignment, enter the date and the assignment on his page in the notebook. Beneath the entry, have the student write why he was unable to turn in his homework as assigned. The excuse book makes students accountable for their homework and it provides excellent documentation when conferring with students and their parents. You're sure to get some unusual excuses, but fewer and fewer students will be forgetting their homework!

Susan Shaw, John Baker Elementary School, Albuquerque, NM

Homework Help

Taking a weekly approach to homework assignments benefits students and you! On Monday send home a form like the one shown that lists the homework assignments for the week. Then, on Friday, collect the students' homework along with their parent-signed assignment sheets. Students (and their parents) appreciate the flexibility of this approach, and you'll find that you spend less time checking homework. In addition, you have a ready-to-file record of each child's weekly homework efforts.

Angela Story
Cedar Road Elementary
Chesapeake, VA

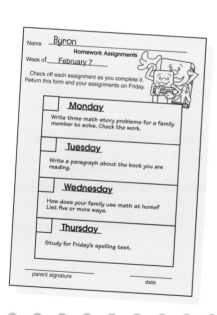

Name Byron
Homework Assignments
Week of February 7

Check off each assignment as you complete it.
Return this form and your assignments on Friday.

Monday
Write three math story problems for a family member to solve. Check the work.

Tuesday
Write a paragraph about the book you are reading.

Wednesday
How does your family use math at home? List five or more ways.

Thursday
Study for Friday's spelling test.

parent signature   date

Assignments at a Glance

Keep students aware of upcoming assignments and test dates with this visual reminder. Laminate a large calendar grid and post it on a bulletin board or wall. Each month, use a wipe-off marker to program the calendar with the month, dates, and other desired information. At a glance, students can see when assignments are due and tests will be given. At the end of the month, wipe away the programming and repeat the procedure for the succeeding month.

Ana L. Wilson
Berwyn, IL

MARCH

M	T	W	T	F	S	S
1	2	3 Map Due!	4	5 Spelling Test	6	7
8	9	10	11	12 Spelling Test	13	14
15	16	17	18	19 Spelling Test	20	21
22	23	24 Science Project Due	25	26 Spelling Test	27	28
29	30	31 Share Book Projects				

Brownie Points

This tasty incentive program motivates youngsters to be the best that they can be. With your students' help, create a list of positive behaviors and/or academic challenges that exceed the established expectations. Assign a point value to each item on the list; then display the list in a prominent classroom location. For added visual appeal, shape a border from aluminum foil to resemble a baking pan. Create a chart on which to record the points the class earns each day. When the class earns a predetermined number of points, reward the students with a freshly baked pan of brownies. If desired, enlist your students' help in making the treat. No doubt these will be the tastiest brownie points your students have ever earned!

Brenda Martin
Baty Elementary School, Del Valle, TX

How To Earn Brownie Points

Extra Efforts:	Points:
Write an article for the school paper.	5 points
Complete an extra book report.	5 points
Introduce a new vocabulary word to the class.	5 points
Volunteer to help another child, teacher, or class.	5 points
Earn a class star in music, library, or P.E. class.	5 points
Earn a compliment from an adult.	5 points

Follow-up Folder

Providing individualized instruction just got easier! Keep a file folder labeled "Follow-up Needed" on your desk. When a child's completed work indicates that he needs additional help with a skill, file his paper in the folder. Each time you have a few free minutes, select a paper from the folder and meet with the corresponding youngster. Spare minutes quickly become teachable moments!

Gina Marinelli
Bernice Young Elementary
Burlington, NJ

Follow-up Needed

Your Name, Please

Tired of reminding your students to put their names on their papers? Teach your students a clever chant like "Put your N-A-M-E on the T-O-P." Or challenge students to create their own classroom chant as a handy reminder not to forget to write their names on their papers. Presto—no more nameless papers!

Letita Thompson
Derby Ridge Elementary
Columbia, MO

Record-Keeping Calendars

Tracking students' work habits just got easier! Make a construction paper folder for each child and mount a duplicated calendar page on the front of it. Each day have students store their completed assignments inside their folders. Every afternoon remove the contents of each child's folder. If an assignment is missing, note it in the calendar space for that day. If all work has been completed, stamp the space with a seasonal stamper. At the end of the month, document each child's work habits in your gradebook; then send the folders home. A parent is sure to appreciate this visual record of his or her child's monthly work habits.

Kellie Provost
Arroyo Mocho Elementary, Livermore, CA

Early Finishers

To prepare for students who finish their work early, place dot-to-dots, word finds, crossword puzzles, and leftover skill pages in a designated box. When a student finishes an assignment early, he chooses an activity from the box to complete. Your early finishers will be busy, which makes them less likely to distract other classmates who are trying to finish their work. And you'll be free to focus on students who need your help.

Wendy Goodman
Montclaire Elementary
Charlotte, NC

Family Matters

Minimize the problem of nameless assignments with this proven method. Arrange your students' desks into groups called *families*. After distributing daily assignments, family members encourage one another to write their names on their papers. After a designated amount of time, each family that has completed this task earns a point. Reward each family after it earns a predetermined number of points.

Penny Blazer
Penns Valley School District
Spring Mills, PA

Promoting Quality Work

This incentive program motivates students to carefully complete their work. Each student needs a personalized punch card like the one shown. A student earns one punch for each perfect paper that he completes. (For easy management, post the times during which you are available to punch students' cards.) When all of the punches on a child's card have been removed, he exchanges his card for a new one and receives a small prize. If desired, compile your youngsters' completed punch cards on a shower ring. When 50 cards have been collected, reward the entire class with a special treat or privilege.

Judy Janzen
Joshua Independent School District
Joshua, TX

Game Management

Keep track of the many games your youngsters complete with this motivating, star-studded idea. Store your manipulative games in a box and place the box on a table. Supply each child with an index card programmed with circles labeled to correspond with the games. Each time a student completes a game from the box, put a star in the corresponding circle and write the date above it. Encourage each student to complete as many games as he wishes in the allotted time. When a child gets all of his circles starred, provide him with a new card; then reward him with a treat or star sticker.

Lori O'Malley
Dingman Delaware Elementary School
Dingmans Ferry, PA

Ask Three Before You Ask Me

Put a familiar phrase to good use as students take responsibility for their own learning. Post the phrase "Ask Three Before You Ask Me" in a prominent location as a reminder for students. Tell your youngsters that if they have a question, they should ask three other students before asking you. Before a child asks you a question, have him name the three students he's already asked. Students will create an atmosphere of cooperation, and you'll minimize the number of times you repeat directions!

Cheryl A. Wade
Golden Springs Elementary
Oxford, AL

Good-Work Tickets

Motivate your youngsters with these good-work tickets. To make the tickets, program a large supply of index cards with dots along the top and bottom edges. (Adjust the number of dots according to your students' needs.) Write a different child's name on each card; then distribute the cards. When a child completes an assignment or demonstrates good behavior, use a hole puncher to punch out one of the dots on his ticket. When all of the dots have been punched, the child may turn his ticket in for a preestablished reward such as a trip to the prize box.

Karen Saner
Burns Elementary
Burns, KS

Clip It!

Use clipboards to organize students' work and school papers. For each child, provide a clipboard that has a hole for hanging it up. Mount hanging hooks in a pegboard; then label each place with a child's name. When students arrive in the morning, request that they hang their clipboards on the hooks. Throughout the day, teachers and students can clip papers onto the clipboards as needed. At the end of the day, packing up is quick and easy because each child's papers are all in one place. Parents can also use the clipboard to send papers or messages back to you. It's easy—just clip it!

Martha Ann Davis, Pinecrest Elementary, Greenwood, SC

Nameless Papers

Enlist your students' help in putting an end to nameless papers. Give each group (or row) of students a paper cup that is to be displayed on a different group member's desk each day. Before an assignment is turned in, the student with the cup on his desk verifies that all papers in his group have names. Each time a group successfully submits only papers with names, place a wooden craft stick in its cup. When a group has earned a designated number of craft sticks, present its members with a special reward or privilege.

Kay A. Fuller
Clearview Elementary School
Brogue, PA

Nifty Neatness Awards

I use Nifty Neatness Awards to encourage neat work in my class. Students know that each day (or every other day), one assignment is eligible for Nifty Neatness Awards—but they aren't sure which one. I secretly choose one set of papers from all of the assignments I collect. Each student who completes that assignment neatly is awarded a neatness certificate, which I staple to the top of his paper. When papers are returned, students remove their awards and save them. After earning ten awards, a student is eligible for one of a variety of privileges such as skipping an assignment, being the teacher's helper for the day, or having extra free time.

Dianne Neumann
Frank C. Whiteley School
Hoffman Estates, IL

Official Encourager

Each day assign one student in your class to be the "official encourager." Her job for the entire day is to look for students who are excelling in any given area, and to give each one a friendly pat on the back. The pat can be a real one or a small card that says, "Give yourself a pat on the back. You deserve it!"

Cindy Lonergan—Special Education, Disney Elementary, Tulsa, OK

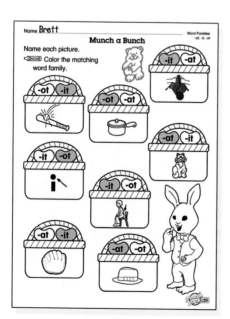

Bear Stamping

A tiny bear encourages my students to do their very best work! When grading papers, I look for students who have tried a little harder to do their best writing or coloring. For some students, completing an assignment is a noteworthy accomplishment. I stamp those papers with a bear stamp. A student who earns a bear knows that he will also receive a small reward. Students can't wait to look at their papers to see if they've earned any bear stamps!

Lynn Maxey
Oklahoma Union Elementary
Lenapah, OK

Absent Folders

Here's a "grape" way to keep track of a student's make-up work. Program a copy of an open reproducible; then duplicate it to make a supply of assignment sheets. Store the copies in a convenient classroom location. When a student is absent, write his name and the date on a copy of the assignment sheet. Throughout the day, write in the appropriate space on the sheet each assignment that needs to be made up. Put the programmed sheet into a colorful folder and set it on the student's desk. When the student returns to school, he completes the assignments he missed. When he finishes an assignment, he checks it off his assignment sheet, and then he places his completed work in the colorful folder. When his make-up work is completed, he returns the folder, along with the assignment sheet, to you. If desired, request that the student's parents review the make-up work and sign the assignment sheet.

Shannon Berry
Algoma Christian School, Kent City, MI

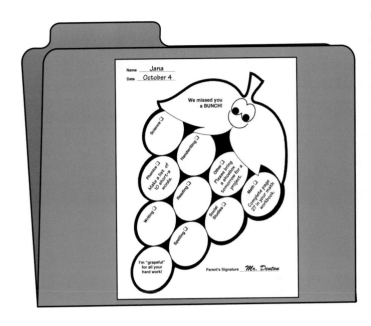

Paper of the Day

Encourage students to carefully complete their work with this paper-of-the-day plan. Conclude each day by presenting one outstanding assignment that was completed that day. Enlist your students' help in identifying the positive qualities of the paper such as neatness, accuracy, originality, and completeness. Then showcase the paper in a special frame designed for this purpose. A round of applause for the proud owner of the paper of the day is definitely in order!

Debbie Byrne, Candor Elementary, Candor, NY

Absent Folders

Use these colorful file folders to organize work for students who are absent. Label each of several folders "Absent Folder"; then write a cheery message on each one. Laminate the folders for durability; then store them in a convenient location. When a student is absent, place an "Absent Folder" on his desk. Ask a student helper to place the absent student's assignments in the folder throughout the day. When a parent or sibling comes to retrieve the student's work, or when the student returns to school, the missed assignments are in one handy location.

Tricia Peña, Acacia Elementary, Vail, AZ

Individualized Assistance

Take a tip from your local baker when devising a plan for meeting with individual students. Hole-punch a class set of index cards and number them consecutively. Place the cards in numerical order on a hook attached to the front of your desk. A student seeking your assistance takes a number, knowing she'll have your undivided attention when her number is called. Or distribute numbers to those students you wish to meet with to provide instruction, encouragement, or positive feedback. Next!

Carol Ann Perks
Comstock Elementary
Miami, FL

...And You Never Miss a Beat

To cut down on interruptions from children requesting permission to go to the rest room, encourage each child to simply raise two fingers (like a peace sign) to indicate her need. Then you can acknowledge each request by a simple nod of your head and go right on teaching.

Betsy Gignac
St. John the Evangelist
Watertown, CT

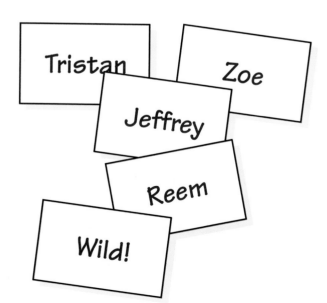

Random Responses

Keep students tuned in and ready to participate with a customized card deck! Personalize one index card per child and label two more cards "Wild." To use the card deck (for class discussions, large-group reviews, etc.), shuffle it, and then draw cards one by one, calling upon the corresponding students. When a Wild card is drawn, the student who answered the previous question answers again or chooses a classmate to answer. Regularly shuffle the deck to keep everyone tuned in! It's a great deal of fun!

Sister Maribeth Theis
Mary of Lourdes Elementary
Little Falls, MN

Communication

Contents

Snack Pack

Are you having trouble getting donated snacks delivered to school on the day that they're needed? Here's a tip that offers a little celebrity and motivation to your snack carriers. In advance, use fabric paints to decorate one or more canvas tote bags. In the bag's art, include your name and grade so the bag can be returned if it gets misplaced. The day before a child is scheduled to bring in a snack, present him with the bag. Instruct him to bring the snack to school in the bag the next day. Youngsters will soon be motivated by the honor of responsibility!

Karin Vorheis
Spring Lake Elementary
Ocoee, FL

Partnering With Parents

Here's a solution for parents who want to volunteer but are unable to help during school hours. Prepare packets with simple assignments and have parents complete them at home! To make one packet, write the directions and the due date for the assignment on a sheet of paper; then staple the paper to a large manila envelope. Fill the envelope with all the necessary materials to complete the assignment. Send the packet home with the child and have him return it to school when completed.

Ginny Haithcock, George Hall Elementary, Mobile, AL

I Got Your Note!

To ensure that you receive and keep track of parents' notes, have them slip 'em in the mailbox. Position a decorated mailbox in a spot near your door. When parents have notes for you, ask them to place them in the mailbox and raise the flag. Then there they'll be—ready when you are!

Libby Anne Inabinet
Eastminster Day School
Columbia, SC

Notes? No Problem!

Sending personalized notes home to parents is a snap with this idea! For each child's parent, program and sign a supply of decorative note sheets. Then file all the note sheets by name in a file box with A–Z dividers. When you observe a student doing something worth sharing, grab one of his personalized note sheets and jot down a quick message. The note is ready to go in just seconds! This system not only saves time, but also allows you to see which parents have not yet received positive news.

Rhonda Foster
West Central Elementary School
Francesville, IN

Keep in Touch

If your school has a voice-mail system, here's an idea to make that modern technology work for you! Record an outgoing message on your voice mail, telling parents of your week's activities and upcoming studies. Also be sure to mention any special events or accomplishments. In your weekly newsletter, publish your voice-mail number. Encourage parents to call the number whenever they'd like to find out what's going on in your classroom. You can even feature your students as guest reporters on this voice-mail system. Or use it to teach families a new song, or send out a special class holiday greeting. Even if you can't come to the phone, the phone can speak for you!

Nancy Nason Biddinger, Little River Elementary, Orlando, FL

Ready to Reply

Do you sometimes have trouble getting children's parents to reply to written communications? Here's a tip that seems to help. When you send a note home that requests a parent to reply, attach a decorative sticky note—the fancier, the better! With the attractive paper right on hand, they are more likely to write a reply then and there.

Kathleen Hunter
Tara Elementary
Morrow, GA

Keeping Up With Correspondence

Managing parent correspondence can seem like a full-time job. Make the task easier with this handy parent communication binder. Purchase a large three-ring binder and a class supply of pocket dividers. Label one pocket for each student. Also complete a student information sheet for each child. Place each child's information sheet and pocket folder side by side in your binder. Each time you receive a written message from a parent, file it in the appropriate pocket. And if you wish to respond to a parent, the information you need is right at your fingertips.

Anna Kellum
Forest Hills Elementary
Walterboro, SC

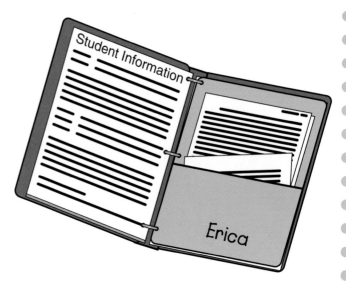

Friday Folders

To help make communication with parents a simple task, use Friday folders. Supply each child with a personalized two-pocket folder. Each Friday place newsletters, calendars (highlighting special events and dates), rewards, and memos in the folders; then have each child take his folder home. Encourage each youngster to return his folder on Monday so it can be reused the next week. Parents will love getting their weekly special deliveries and being kept up on all the news.

Reneé Martin, Westwood Hills Elementary School, Waynesboro, VA

The ABCs of Kindergarten

Inform parents about the basics of kindergarten with this unique welcome-to-school booklet. Organize an alphabetical list of information that you would like parents to know, such as school policies and classroom procedures. Type the information; then make copies to present to each parent during orientation sessions or parent conferences. Parents are sure to appreciate this valuable resource that they can refer to throughout the year.

Kathleen Miller
Our Lady of Mt. Carmel School
Tenafly, NJ

Class Address Book

Keep students' phone numbers and addresses at your fingertips with this suggestion. At the beginning of the year, record each child's home information in an inexpensive address book. Keep the book conveniently located near your phone at home. In this book, you'll also be able to record the date and topic of phone conversations as they take place. At the end of the year, enclose the book and a class picture in an envelope for your records.

Patt Hall
Babson Park Elementary
Lake Wales, FL

PTA Reminders

It's easy for parents to forget about a PTA meeting, even though reminders are sent home ahead of time. One way to increase parent participation is to call each child's home to personally invite the parents. Another last-minute reminder can be delivered on the day of the meeting. Before each student leaves for the day, loosely tie a ribbon around one of his fingers. Explain that the ribbon is a reminder to him to remind his parents that this is PTA day.

Patt Hall

Paper Trail Notebook

Here's a simple system for tracking assorted parent correspondence, from field trip permission forms to conference slips to requests for supplies. Prepare a class list (or two), leaving blank space at the top of each list for a title. Keep a supply of the lists in a notebook at your desk. To track returned correspondence, appropriately title a class list and then mark out each child's name as you receive her paperwork. Circle the name of any student who forgets her paperwork and follow up with her. If your record keeping reveals that select students routinely need reminders, address the issue with the youngsters and their parents.

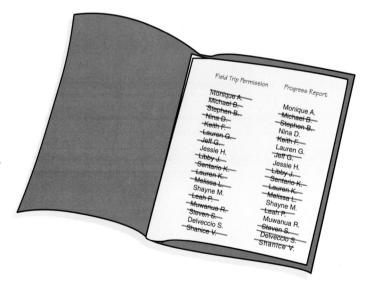

Nancy Long
Washington-Wilkes Primary School
Washington, GA

Stick-On Reminders

These special reminders are sure to make it home with your youngsters. Use colorful markers to program self-adhesive labels with important messages. Press a label onto a youngster's shirt for a reminder that won't be missed by his parents!

Barb Hunt
Kinderhouse
Cedarville, OH

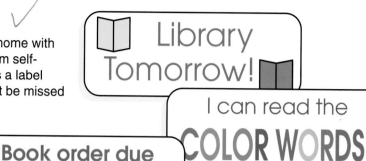

Library Tomorrow!

I can read the COLOR WORDS.

Book order due tomorrow.

Date Stamp

Do you like to show parents the progress in their children's work? Try this timesaving tip. As a child finishes a paper or project, stamp the date on it with a date stamp. Now his work can easily be chronologically organized, and a parent can see his child's progress at a glance.

Beth Myer, Lincoln School, Ottawa, IL

Dustin
Ms. Ward's Class

Parent Pockets

Here's an idea to ensure that important papers get from school to home—and back again! For each child, label a large string-tie envelope with his name and class. Encourage each child to decorate his envelope; then laminate the envelopes. Cut along each envelope's flap with an X-acto knife. Presto! Parent pockets are a practical, portable, water-resistant means of transporting communications between home and school.

Karin Thompson
Conley School
Bethlehem Township, NJ

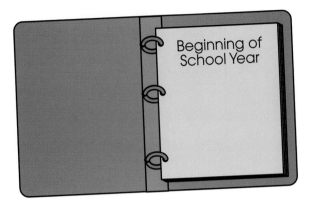

Organizing Important Letters

Locating important letters and handouts for parents is a breeze with this timesaving idea. Label one pocket folder for each of these topics: beginning of the school year, end of the school year, conferences, articles, report cards, invitations, permission slips, and miscellaneous. Hole-punch the folders and place them in a large, three-ring binder. Keep original copies of letters and handouts for parents in the folders. At the beginning of the month, browse through the folders and duplicate the items you need. Locating needed materials has never been easier!

Linh Tran, Charles B. Wallace Elementary, York, PA

Student Information Notebook

Record important student information and document parent communications in this one-of-a-kind notebook. On individual pages in a spiral notebook, write your students' names in alphabetical order. Allow one or more blank pages between each entry. On each personalized page, list the student's date of birth, home address, and home phone number. Also list the name of each parent and a daytime phone number where he or she can be reached. If desired, list an emergency contact person and note any allergies the student may have. Throughout the year, record all parent communications in the notebook. List the date, the time, and a brief description of the communication (phone call, written note, conference). Record the nature and outcome of each contact. This thorough method of documentation becomes a great reference throughout the year.

MaryAnne Marshall, Orange, NJ

Charting a Course Toward Better Communication

Maintain a record of positive parent-teacher communications with this handy chart. On a sheet of paper, list your students' names in a column to the left. Draw lines to make three or more additional columns. Label the columns with headings such as "Phone Call," "Good News Gram," "Postcard," and "Personal Contact." Each time you have positive communication with a parent about his or her child, note the date and the reason for the contact in the appropriate column on the chart. A quick glance at the chart reveals who needs to hear from you next! Make a new chart at the beginning of each grading period.

Kristyn Haberkorn
Greenvale Park Elementary
Northfield, MN

Positive Parent-Teacher Communications

Student	Phone Call	Good News Gram	Postcard	Personal Contact
Beatrice		12/8 Time Test		1/4 Science Project
Cathy	12/5 Behavior		1/9 Homework	

Special Delivery Envelopes

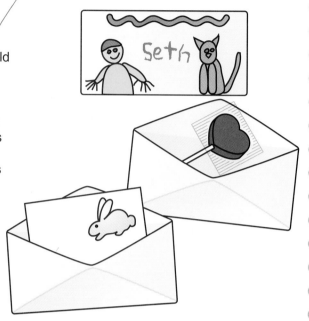

This special mail call provides a fun way to stay organized. After all, who doesn't love getting mail? To begin, give each child a business-size envelope and have him print his name on the front. Then encourage each child to decorate his envelope as desired. Store the completed envelopes in a mailbox. For special occasions, simply slide a note of praise or a seasonal treat in each child's envelope. To give a special assignment (such as a classroom job or center assignment), slip a note, picture, or photo depicting the desired event into the corresponding child's envelope. As an added bonus, these handy missives can also be used as place cards to assign seats during snacktimes and mealtimes. Your little ones will enjoy receiving their mail!

Beulah F. Cordell
An Academe for Children
Springdale, AR

End-of-the-Day Reminder

Do you sometimes forget things you should remind students of at the end of the day? If so, then write "Please Remember" at the top of a sheet of poster board. Color, decorate, and laminate the poster. Attach a length of string to a corner, and tie a wipe-off marker to the end of the string. Tape the poster to the inside of your classroom door. During the day, as you think of things that students will need to be reminded of, write them on the poster with the wipe-off marker. At the end of the day, refer to the "Please Remember" reminder before sending students home.

Jeanette N. Allen, Cottonwood, AZ

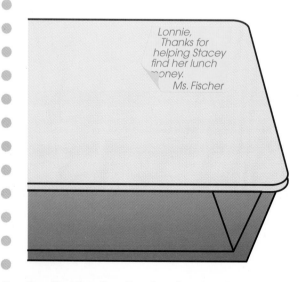

Lonnie,
Thanks for helping Stacey find her lunch money.
Ms. Fischer

Notes of Praise

Boost your youngsters' self-esteem and encourage positive behavior with these simple notes of praise. Keep a supply of Post-it notes handy throughout the day. Each time a youngster exhibits praiseworthy behavior, note his actions on a Post-it note. When your students leave the room for recess or a special activity, attach the notes to the appropriate desks.

Christine Fischer
George J. Peters School
Cranston, RI

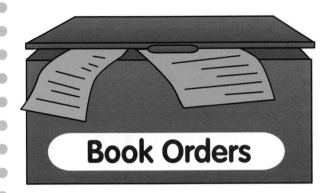

Book Order Box

This idea helps keep book orders from being misplaced. Set a plastic school box labeled "Book Orders" on your desk. When students return their orders to school, have them place their orders and money in the box. After mailing your class order, return the order forms to the box until the books arrive.

Jan Tschritter
Linton Elementary
Linton, ND

Remember Your Book Orders!

Here's an effective way to remind students when book orders are due. On your class calendar, attach a book-shaped cutout on the due date. At a glance, students can see the deadline for book orders.

Stephanie Speicher
Elm Road Elementary School
Mishawaka, IN

Signing Out and In

This classroom checkout system is a timesaver and a teaching tool. Each morning post a daily sign-out sheet like the one shown. When a student needs to leave the classroom, she signs the sheet and records the time. Then, when she returns to the classroom, she records the current time. You'll spend fewer minutes monitoring the classroom door and your students' time-telling skills are sure to improve. As an added bonus, you have documentation of the frequency in which students exit the classroom.

Sue Lorey
Arlington Heights, IL

What's the Time?

Name	Out	In
Katie	8:30	8:34
Ben	8:52	8:57
Caroline	9:15	9:21
Danielle	9:30	9:36
Nicholas	10:06	10:11
Stacie	10:20	8:24

Wristband Reminders

Remind students and parents of upcoming events with wristband reminders. Keep a supply of 8½" x 1" paper strips on hand. When you wish to send a reminder home, write the desired message on the chalkboard and have each student copy the message onto a paper strip. Ask each child to wrap his resulting reminder around his wrist so that you can tape or staple the ends of the strip together. These nifty reminders are the perfect fit for any occasion!

Tara Murphy
Oconee County Primary School
Watkinsville, GA

Field trip tomorrow. Bring your lunch

Pocketing Papers ✓

Help students organize take-home papers with pocket folders. Personalize and label a two-pocket folder for each child. Ask students to store the folders in their desks during the day and then take the folders home each afternoon. Whenever you distribute items that are to be taken home (graded papers, announcements, notes to parents), designate in which folder pocket each item should be placed. Parents can quickly see which papers are to be kept, and which ones need to be read and returned to school in the folder. Parents will appreciate this organized approach, and you'll spend less time tracking down missing correspondence.

Bernadette Burns
High Bridge Elementary School
High Bridge, NJ

Bagged And Ready To Go

Here's a quick and simple way to keep a student's take-home papers all together, dry, and clean! For each child, provide a gallon-size resealable plastic bag. With a permanent marker, write his name on the bag. At the end of each day, place the child's take-home papers in the bag, seal it, and then send it home with him. Encourage the child to return papers and other belongings in his bag the following day.

Jo-Ellen Forrest
Hickey School
St. Louis, MO

Cubby Alternative

Here's a space-saving alternative when cubbies are not available. For each child, glue a construction paper mailbox onto a manila envelope. Then glue on construction paper crayons to resemble the mailbox stand. Fold the tab inside the envelope; then laminate the envelope. Slit across the top of the envelope with a razor blade. Use a brad to attach a construction paper mailbox flag to the top layer of the envelope. Then use a permanent marker to write the child's name on the mailbox. Explain that whenever a child has papers to take home, the flag will be raised—by either you or the child. When he removes his papers at the end of the day, he slides the flag down. This enables you to tell at a glance who might still need to collect his take-home papers.

Daphne M. Orenshein
Yavneh Hebrew Academy
Los Angeles, CA

Schoolwide Memos

If your school saves paper by sending home schoolwide memos with just the oldest child in each represented family, try this! Attach a colorful sticker dot to the desk of each child who is to receive the paperwork. Then send home schoolwide memos with students who have the dots on their desks. Distributing papers by the dots definitely saves time!

Kelly Hanover
Saint Edward School
Racine, WI

The Messenger

Help strengthen the home-school connection with these handy homework carriers. For each child, label the left side of a two-pocket folder "Return to School." Label the right side "Completed." Put finished student work and notes in the right side. Place homework and papers that need to be returned to school in the left side. Encourage responsibility by having each child bring his folder to and from school every day. As children arrive, have them place their folders in a designated basket. You can quickly look through the folders to retrieve any returned papers or other homework communications.

Debbie Perry
St. Brigid School
Midland, MI

The Talking Stick

To keep your sharing times fair, use the Talking Stick. The stick can be a ruler, a dowel, or a piece of interesting wood. Only the person holding the stick may talk at that specific time. Be sure that the Talking Stick is passed to each child so that everyone has a chance to share.

Andrea M. Troisi
LaSalle Middle School
Niagara Falls, NY

Taking Papers Home

Save precious class time by sending home corrected student work once a week. Have each child personalize the front of a file folder. Laminate the folders for durability and tape a parent response sheet, like the one shown, inside each one. Once a week, set aside a few minutes to distribute the folders and your students' corrected work. Each child carries his papers home inside his folder. A parent removes and reviews the contents of the folder; then he or she dates, signs, and adds a comment to the response sheet. The following school day the student returns the empty folder. Each week you'll save time and communicate with parents!

Tomara Steadman
St. Marks Elementary
Colwich, KS

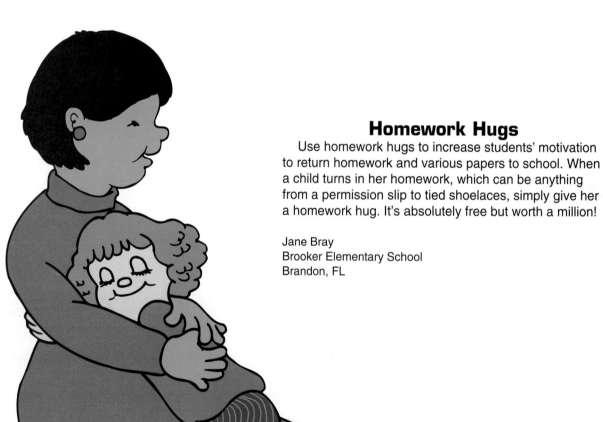

Homework Hugs

Use homework hugs to increase students' motivation to return homework and various papers to school. When a child turns in her homework, which can be anything from a permission slip to tied shoelaces, simply give her a homework hug. It's absolutely free but worth a million!

Jane Bray
Brooker Elementary School
Brandon, FL

Fantastic Folders

Help your youngsters organize their papers with this simple pocket-folder system. Have each student bring three pocket folders to school. Collect one of the folders and store it as a replacement. Have each student label and decorate one folder "Stay at School" and another folder "Take Home." Explain to your students that schoolwork for collection at the end of each day should be placed in their "Stay At School" folders. Papers that need to be taken home should be placed in their "Take Home" folders for review with a parent each night. (You may choose to include a parent sign-off sheet in each "Take Home" folder.) Parents and students will agree—this organized approach is fantastic!

Margie Siegel
Wren Hollow Elementary School
Ballwin, MO

Ribbon Reminders

These colorful reminders help students and parents identify important notices and assignments. Before sending home an important paper, have each child use a hole puncher to punch a hole in the top of the page. Then have the child thread a length of curling ribbon through the hole and tie a bow. The bow serves as an eye-catching reminder that the paper needs special attention. If desired, devise a color-coded ribbon system for important papers such as:

red = school announcements, forms, or special events

green = homework or extra practice assignments

gold = fantastic work

Jeanine Peterson
Bainbridge Elementary
Bainbridge, IN

I like going camping with my Dad.

Oops! Notice

How often have you heard the phrase "Oops! I forgot!" when collecting homework assignments? These reminder notices are an effective way to foster responsibility in your students. Make a supply of notices like the one shown. Each time a student forgets to turn in a homework assignment, have him complete and carry home a notice that must be returned with a parent signature the following school day. With this homework plan in place, forgotten homework could soon be a thing of the past!

Patricia Dent
Kindle School
Pitman, NJ

Right on Time

How many times have you forgotten to ready a student for early pickup? Try this! Place a manipulative clock on the student's desk; then, with the student's help, program it to show a time that is five minutes before his parent is scheduled to arrive. When the times on the class clock and the manipulative clock match, the youngster clears his desk and gathers his things. His actions will prompt you to take care of other necessary preparations, and by the time his parent arrives, the child will be ready to go!

Rita Yanoff
Sussex Christian School
Hope, NJ